WRITING ON TRIAL:
TIMOTHY FINDLEY'S *FAMOUS LAST WORDS*

Canadian Fiction Studies

Additional volumes are available

Writing on Trial:
TIMOTHY FINDLEY'S

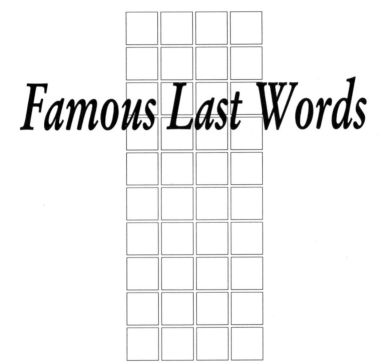

Famous Last Words

Diana Brydon

E C W P R E S S

CANADIAN CATALOGUING IN PUBLICATION DATA

Brydon, Diana, 1950–
"Writing on trial" : Timothy Findley's
Famous last words

(Canadian fiction studies ; 32)
Includes bibliographical references and index.
ISBN 1-55022-181-7
1. Findley, Timothy, 1930– . Famous Last Words.
1. Title. 11. Series.

PS8511.I38F3433 1995   C813'.54   C95-930405-3
PR9199.3.F55F3433 1995

This book has been published with the assistance of the
Ministry of Culture, Recreation and Tourism of the Province
of Ontario, through funds provided by the Ontario
Publishing Centre, and with the assistance of grants from
The Canada Council, the Ontario Arts Council, and the
Government of Canada through the Department of
Canadian Heritage, and the Canadian Studies and Special Projects
Directorate of the Department of the Secretary of State of Canada.

The cover features a reproduction of the dust-wrapper
from the first edition of *Famous Last Words*, courtesy of the
Thomas Fisher Rare Book Library, University of Toronto.
Frontispiece photograph by Elisabeth Feryn,
reproduced by permission.
Design and imaging by ECW Type & Art, Oakville, Ontario.
Printed by Imprimerie d'Édition Marquis, Montmagny, Quebec.

Distributed by General Distribution Services,
30 Lesmill Road, Don Mills, Ontario M3B 2T6.

Published by ECW PRESS,
2120 Queen Street East,
Toronto, Ontario M4E 1E2.

Table of Contents

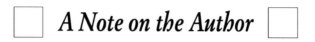

A Note on the Author

Diana Brydon teaches Canadian and postcolonial literatures at the University of Guelph. She is the author of *Christina Stead* (Macmillan, 1987) and the coauthor, with Helen Tiffin, of *Decolonising Fictions* (Dangaroo, 1993); editor of the Canadian section of the *Encyclopedia of Postcolonial Literatures in English*; and guest editor of a forthcoming special issue of *Essays on Canadian Writing* entitled *Postcolonial Theories and Canadian Literatures*. Her current project is a book on the intersections of feminism and postcolonialism in relation to reinscriptions of Shakespeare's *The Tempest*.

NOTE ON REFERENCES AND ACKNOWLEDGEMENT

The text of *Famous Last Words* to which I refer throughout is the original 1981 Canadian edition published by Clarke, Irwin, and Company.

I would like to acknowledge a research grant from the Social Sciences and Humanities Research Council of Canada that enabled me to complete this project, and the research assistance of Nima Naghibi.

Writing on Trial:
Timothy Findley's
Famous Last Words

Chronology

1930   Timothy Findley born 30 October in Toronto.

1945   Graduates from Rosedale Public School, Toronto.

1945–48   Secondary education at Jarvis Collegiate, Toronto. In and out of school until he leaves at age sixteen.

1953   Becomes a charter member of the Stratford Shakespearean Festival.

1956   "About Effie," first published short story, appears in *Tamarack Review*.

1957–58   Lives in Hollywood, California, and writes for CBS.

1964   Moves to Stone Orchard Farm in Cannington, Ontario, with partner William Whitehead.

1967   *The Last of the Crazy People.*
The Paper People televised on CBC.

1969   *The Butterfly Plague.*
Writes screenplay for the NFB film, *Don't Let the Angels Fall.*

1971–72   Seven scripts, *The Whiteoaks of Jalna*, televised on CBC. Wins Armstrong Radio Drama Award for *The Journey*, 1971.

1974   Eight scripts by Findley and Whitehead, *The National Dream*, televised on CBC.

1974–75   Writes, as playwright in residence at the National Arts Centre, Ottawa, *Can You See Me Yet?*
Receives, with Whitehead, ACTRA Best Documentary Writer Award for *The National Dream*, 1975.

1976   *Can You See Me Yet?* produced at the National Arts Centre (premières 1 March).

1977	*The Wars*; wins City of Toronto Book Award and Governor General's Literary Award. *Can You See Me Yet?* published.
1977–78	Chairman of The Writers' Union of Canada.
1978	Receives Author of the Year award from the Periodical Distributors of Canada.
1978–79	Writer in residence at the University of Toronto.
1979	*John A. — Himself!* produced at Theatre London, London, Ontario (premières 31 January). *Dieppe, 1942*, by Findley and Whitehead, broadcast on CBC Radio; wins ANIK Best Documentary Award.
1980	*Other People's Children* and *Songs*, three scripts, broadcast on CBC Radio.
1981	*Famous Last Words.*
1982	Receives honorary D.Litt. from Trent University.
1983	Screenplay of *The Wars* for the NFB. Receives Author of the Year award from the Periodical Distributors of Canada.
1984	*Dinner along the Amazon.* *Not Wanted on the Voyage.* Wins Author of the Year award from the Canadian Booksellers Association. Also wins Author of the Year award from the Periodical Distributors of Canada. Receives honorary D.Litt. from the University of Guelph.
1985	Wins Canadian Authors Association Literary Award for *Not Wanted on the Voyage.*
1986	*The Butterfly Plague* (revised edition). Becomes Officer of the Order of Canada. Wins CNIB Talking Book of the Year Award for *Not Wanted on the Voyage.* Receives Periodical Marketers of Canada Award for *Not Wanted on the Voyage.*
1986–87	President, English-Canadian centre, of P.E.N. International.
1987	Receives Foundation for the Advancement of Canadian Letters and Periodical Marketers of Canada Annual

Award for *The Telling of Lies.*

1988   *Stones.*
Famous Last Words produced in five parts on CBC Radio; Findley wrote adaptation and performed in it.

1989   Wins Trillium Award for *Stones.*
Wins Edgar Award for *The Telling of Lies.*
Wins National Radio Award for adaptation of *Famous Last Words.*

1990   *Inside Memory: Pages from a Writer's Workbook.*

1991   Named to the Order of Ontario.

1993   *Headhunter.*
The Stillborn Lover; produced at the Grand Theatre in London, Ontario.

The Importance of the Work

Timothy Findley describes *Famous Last Words* as "a book that is written on the walls of a hotel by a novelist under threat of death" (*Inside Memory* 193). That novelist, Hugh Selwyn Mauberley, has been condemned — without a trial — because of the power of what he has written and may still write. Findley believes that literature should never be censored because its value lies in testing limits and putting the assumptions of civilization itself on trial. But to deny censorship is not to deny scrutiny. In that sense, literature is always on trial, for it is where the human imagination renews itself. Without attention, literature will die. The metaphor of the trial, in this sense of giving a text attention of the gravest kind, shapes this complex book.

Famous Last Words provides the trial that Mauberley's writing never gets by reproducing his writing within various frames that establish the history of its production and reception. His act of remembering history and reordering it into a narrative puts history on trial. But history itself also tries him: as Fascist collaborator and as writer. Although Mauberley's killer denies him a proper trial, Mauberley puts himself on trial in the story that he tells; he is tried by his readers within the story; and he is tried again by each of us as we try to make sense of his story. The novel asks for each of us as readers to exercise our own judgement as we proceed through this mock trial, but it also asks for our understanding and compassion.

Since the Iranian *fatwah* of 14 February 1989 demanding Salman Rushdie's death, questions of artistic freedom and the role of the writer have seemed increasingly urgent. Findley begins the chapter of his memoir devoted to *Famous Last Words* with a moving account of Rushdie's *In Good Faith* and *Is Nothing Sacred?*, texts written partially in response to those who wished to ban *The Satanic Verses* and have Rushdie murdered for writing it. After endorsing Rushdie's argument that, without the freedom to offend, freedom of expression "ceases to exist" (qtd. in *Inside Memory* 187), Findley concludes by praising Rushdie's advocacy of fiction as providing a stage "where the imagination can play out 'all the great debates of society' in ways that society itself forbids" (188). My argument in this book sees *Famous Last Words* as a stage on which we may reenact, with the characters, both the fascination and the horror of fascism in order to understand more clearly the choices facing us today. What is staged for us is a double trial: of literature in the court of life, and of life in the court of literature.

For Findley, books do more than restage debates; they also mediate them: "Books are mediators between our desire and our despair" (*Inside Memory* 188). To extend the trial metaphor, books play the roles of lawyers, of advocate and prosecutor, casting us into each role in turn, but ultimately into the role of judge. *Famous Last Words* restages the debates that led to the Second World War and its conclusion, compelling us to relive these traumatic events, suffering once more the despair brought on by mass destruction, and reliving hopes for peace and alternative endings to humanity's story. Although it is a historical novel, it seems uncannily prophetic in its relevance to the decade that has followed its publication. In 1995, the appeal of fascism is as compelling an issue for understanding as it was during the years leading up to the Second World War.

As a genuine attempt to understand the appeal of fascism to artists and intellectuals, *Famous Last Words* risks offending some of us. Neither the characters (mostly fascists themselves or their sympathizers and collaborators) nor the action (comprising death after death) appeals as mere entertainment, though the writing is much more varied and amusing (usually in sardonic, ironic, or darkly comic ways) than we might suppose from such a serious theme. If there is entertainment to be found here, then it lies in the wordplay, intertextualities, imagery, and energy of the writing itself.

In *Famous Last Words*, writing, as a form of human action, is on trial, but so are we. By our judgements shall we be judged. Each of us must find our own imaginative balance between the despair and the desires released by the text. Findley's own desire compels him to believe passionately that we can refigure the world imaginatively, as both writers and readers, cocreators in the enterprise of remembering history through fiction. Art is valuable, in Findley's view, less as an aesthetic object than as a process, one that enables us to experience imaginatively the full humanity of other people. In reading *Famous Last Words*, we relive these histories, this despair, in order to prepare us to refigure a world more attuned to the needs of our humanity.

Findley sets this collaboration between writer and reader in motion in *Famous Last Words*. Mauberley rewrites his history on the walls and ceilings of four hotel rooms within the larger rewriting that Findley's novel constructs, but those writings and our readings of them enact a remembering of history that is both compelling and ultimately cathartic in its effects. The novel implies that the Second World War cannot be understood in all its horror (and in its redeeming moments of love and courage) without an imaginative reliving of its choices and contradictions through the emotional involvements created by fiction. An intellectual understanding alone is not sufficient for comprehending Findley's belief, as expressed by Walter Benjamin (the great German-Jewish intellectual who died in that war), that "There is no document of civilization which is not at the same time a document of barbarism" (256).

As J.M. Coetzee observes of his own grim novel, *Age of Iron*, detailing the collapse of apartheid South Africa in the 1980s, "What matters is that the contest is staged, that the dead have their say, even those who speak from a totally untenable historical position. So: even in an age of iron, pity is not silenced" (250). I cannot imagine a better summing up of Findley's purpose in *Famous Last Words*. In it, the dead are given their say. If we are to learn the lessons of history, then we need to hear from all participants, even those whose positions we find morally repugnant. Only in understanding them can we hope to defeat them when they challenge our civilization once again, as neofascists and racists are doing right now, in both Europe and North America.

Famous Last Words emphasizes interpretation and the multiple possibilities for making meanings that arise from our individual interactions with its textual constructions of our past. But it also insists that interpretation must lead eventually to judgement, to the taking of a stand, though for each of us that stand may be on different ground. In keeping with contemporary thinking about how literature operates in the world, it downplays the authority of the author and the creativity of artistic genius in order to stress how the making of meaning is always a communal endeavour in which authors and readers struggle to communicate through forms of language and assumptions about language that are not always shared. The book has given rise to diverse interpretations of its meaning and to divergent evaluations of its worth. Most of us would agree, however, that its ambitious range, moral seriousness, and important subject matter guarantee its centrality in contemporary literature.

Critical Reception

When *Famous Last Words* was published in Canada in October 1981, and in the United States the following summer, Timothy Findley already had a reputation as an important Canadian writer, and his newest book was ensured critical scrutiny. The novel was a success with academic critics and general readers alike, garnering largely favourable reviews and selling well. Writing in *Saturday Night*, Barbara Moon reports that Findley was one of the first to benefit from a publisher's bonus given for *Famous Last Words*'s appearance on both the *Maclean's* and the *Toronto Star* best-seller lists. The novel drew attention not only for its substantial achievement as a work of art but also for its audacity in incorporating historical and even living characters into its fictional narrative. Before publication, Findley insured himself against libel charges, knowing that his treatment of the Duchess of Windsor in the novel had the potential to attract such a suit from the litigious duchess. Because of even stricter libel laws in Britain and Europe, his publishers there delayed publication until 1987, a year after the duchess's death. Thus, the threat of libel chill denied Findley access to two large markets for six years.

When the novel finally appeared in the United Kingdom, his treatment of the duchess dominated the reviews, ensuring it notoriety and a place on the best-seller lists but garnering largely negative responses, which Findley sums up in *Inside Memory* as taking the line: *"Who is this colonial hack who has dared to besmirch the memory of our beloved Duchess of Windsor!"* (206). Many reviewers, such as Frank Kermode, an acclaimed expert on Ezra Pound (also a fictionalized character in *Famous Last Words*), took offence at Findley's approach and could not see beyond the perceived insult to Pound and the royal family; others, however, were more measured. Boyd Tonkin in the *New Statesman* makes two important points, about the ways in which *Famous Last Words* expresses "the suspicion and amnesia of the Age of Reagan" and a new kind of nostalgia for lost eras. Similarly, John Gill in *Time Out* discusses the novel as a plausible story of "everyday evil." Writing in the *Times Literary Supplement*, John Melmoth thinks that the novel "takes a long if eventually shifty look at literature's responsibilities." He concludes that the story works as a sophisticated narrative, but fails as an attempt at writing an "alternative history."

American reviews tended to be shorter and more ambivalent than their Canadian counterparts, but they also recognized the importance of the book. Christopher Lehmann-Haupt, in the *New York Times*, praises the book's "extraordinary scenes," which he finds "often strangely beautiful," while remaining more sceptical about the plausibility of the plot. He locates the novel generically as "a new and bizarre form of historical romance." In *Time*, J.D. Reed calls it an "ambitious, disturbing book"; to Ivan Gold, in the *New York Times Book Review*, "It is one hell of a name-dropping story."

Canadian reviewers were also interested in the more sensational fictionalizations of famous people (including the unsolved murder of Sir Harry Oakes, a wealthy Canadian killed in the Bahamas, an incident that, Findley claimed in an interview with Terry Goldie, gave him the idea for the book [62]). But they were also attentive to the book's considerable artistry. These reviews stand up well to the test of time. While impressed by the novel's seriousness of purpose, and sometimes daunted by its scope, several reviewers expressed dissatisfaction with the characterization and the lengthy complexity. They were interested more in the fascism theme than in the meta-fictional elements. Many of the responses, particularly in newspapers across the country, were mixed. Rupert Schieder, in the *Canadian Forum*, speaks for this group of reviewers when he finds the book both "irritating and fascinating."

But others were almost overwhelmingly positive. Keith Garebian focuses on the structure and style, singling out the theatrical effects for special discussion and concluding that the book is a "beautifully haunting triumph of fiction over historical fact" (97). Elspeth Cameron praises Findley's "uncanny descriptive powers" (53), concluding, like Garebian, that "fact ultimately rallies to the side of fiction.

What Findley knows defers always to what he has sensed." She praises *Famous Last Words* as "a novel of the first magnitude: Sophoclean in power, certain in craft, and hauntingly beautiful" (54).

John F. Hulcoop and Eugene Benson, writing in the country's leading academic journals, are equally unstinting in their praise. Benson asserts that Findley has "written only masterpieces" (600), Hulcoop that *Famous Last Words* is "a brave and beautiful book" (121). W.H. New, writing in the *Journal of Commonwealth Literature*, praises the novel for its self-consciously sophisticated and serious investigation into the sources of violence. The Canadian reviews, in both newspapers and learned journals, perceptively identified many of the elements, both aesthetic and ethical, explored at greater length in the articles and books that followed them.

ARTICLES AND CHAPTERS IN BOOKS

The first articles on *Famous Last Words* began to appear in 1984. Writing in the Danish-based postcolonial journal *Kunapipi*, Coral Ann Howells discusses intertextuality and history in *The Wars* and *Famous Last Words*. The intersection of these two concerns has dominated criticism of this novel for the last ten years. Three of the most influential studies appeared in the tenth anniversary issue of *Essays on Canadian Writing* (1984–85). In it, Dennis Duffy, Linda Hutcheon, and Stephen Scobie interrogate elements of Findley's postmodernist technique, including his metafictional play with mythology and history and his involvement of the reader in the moral implications of the narrative. Although Hutcheon's coining of the term "historiographic metafiction" has become the standard terminology for describing Findley's technique in this novel, Duffy's exploration of questions of power and authority, and Scobie's attention to intertextuality and the attraction of fascism, point to important areas of investigation not yet exhausted in the criticism.

Hutcheon expands her insights into Findley's method in several later books, including *A Theory of Parody: The Teachings of Twentieth-Century Art Forms, A Poetics of Postmodernism: History, Theory, Fiction, The Canadian Postmodern: A Study of Contemporary English-Canadian Fiction*, and *The Politics of Postmodernism*. To her,

Findley is clearly a postmodernist writer whose work focuses "in a very self-reflexive way on the processes of both the production and the reception of paradoxically fictive historical writing" (*Politics* 82). Priscilla Walton's article " 'This Isn't a Fairy Tale. . . . It's Mythology': The Colonial Perspective in *Famous Last Words*" elaborates the implications of Hutcheon's postmodernist reading for seeing the novel in postcolonial terms. Walton argues that "the project of Findley's novel is to dramatize the subjectiveness of history, history which has been written from an imperial perspective which excludes those outside that centre" (13). In "Mauberley's Lies: Fact and Fiction in Timothy Findley's *Famous Last Words*," E.F. Shields addresses Findley's blurring of fact and fiction from another angle, concerned less with emphasizing the constructed nature of all written versions of reality than with stressing the importance of discerning the differences between fact and fiction, truth and lies, despite their inevitable confusion. Lorraine M. York also takes up this concern, devoting a few pages of her 1988 book *"The Other Side of Dailiness": Photography in the Works of Alice Munro, Timothy Findley, Michael Ondaatje, and Margaret Laurence* to Findley's use of photographs in *Famous Last Words*. She concentrates on a fictional photograph supposedly of Edward VIII riding in a Daimler at Nice, but actually (within the fiction) of Mauberley hiding behind a newspaper blowup of Edward's smiling face, and on Freyberg's photographs of Dachau, which recall actual photographs, one of which she reproduces in her book.

Elizabeth Seddon pays particular attention to *Famous Last Words* in "The Reader as Actor in the Novels of Timothy Findley." She sees the book as being historical, yet it is "its own self-reflexive commentary on writing, on the role of the writer and on the role of the reader" (217). York's *Front Lines: The Fiction of Timothy Findley* (1991) develops this emphasis on Findley's enabling of the reader more thoroughly in relation to *Famous Last Words*. York reads Findley's entire literary output in terms of metaphors of war. Thus, in discussing *Famous Last Words*, she explores "the notion of reading as ideological warfare" (80). She traces Mauberley's "fall" into fascism, and his subsequent if partial regeneration through his decision to record that fall in writing, as an allegorical counterpart to the "larger historical framework" of "the transition from the 1930s ethos — the rise of fascism — to the 1940s ethos — its repudiation" (89). But in her analysis, what she alternatively calls "the war of aesthetics" and "the war between aesthetics and politics" (91, 95) and the idea of reading as "a field where we do battle with ourselves" (98) take precedence over understanding the political conflicts of the Second World War and the psychic appeal of fascism to the artist.

These interests are raised in several recent works that contest the dominance of readings dependent on Hutcheon's identification of "historiographic metafiction" as the key to understanding *Famous Last Words*. In "Bashing the Fascists: The Moral Dimensions of Findley's Fiction," David Ingham suggests that " 'indirect metafiction' or 'pretend realism' might be more appropriate" terms for understanding Findley's technique (33). His focus falls on fascism as a neglected yet central element in Findley's fiction. Using Findley's comments in interviews, letters, and lectures, he argues that the appeal of Findley's books lies in "their vital connection with the human realities of here and now" (51).

Donna Palmateer Pennee's *Moral Metafiction: Counterdiscourse in the Novels of Timothy Findley* (1991) shares Ingham's interest in the moral dimensions of Findley's vision but accepts the idea that his work is metafictional. Her work develops from her curiosity about Findley's "use of metafictive devices to write about specifically moral issues and morally problematic periods in history" (11). Dissatisfied with the formalist limitations of discussions of historiographic metafiction, she seeks "to go beyond exposing the oppressive operations of power in discourse" (13), "to locate and articulate the mechanics of subversive and affirmative power in discourse" (14). She defines "moral metafiction" (her term) as "fiction 'about' fictions, about the construction of discourses" that is also "driven by a moral imperative to articulate counterdiscourses" (19). Her focus falls on what she calls "the ethical challenge in Findley's novels" (65). This challenge involves her in a discussion of the ways in which *Famous Last Words* recalls insistent themes from Findley's earlier works. This context enables her to identify Mauberley's testament as an exposure of "the horrors of the pursuit" of the fascist ideal (69) and to see Quinn learning to become that text's ideal reader.

In striking contrast to most of the earlier academic critics (but in line with some of the early reviews), David Williams, in *Confessional Fictions: A Portrait of the Artist in the Canadian Novel* (1991), argues that *Famous Last Words* is morally confused. While agreeing with

Pennee that Findley seems to endorse Quinn's sympathetic reading of Mauberley's life, Williams concludes that "... *Famous Last Words* reifies the 'triumph' of beauty over truth by letting the aesthete speak. In that sense, the novel which began as a parody of Pound's attack on the aesthete makes itself a belated target of Pound's great poem" (260). In a complex and carefully documented argument, Williams traces Findley's indebtedness in *Famous Last Words* to the late-nineteenth-century aesthetic movement associated with Pater, Moore, and Wilde. He sees the novel as an example of a work that "fails to transform its models" (36). His argument depends for its force on his careful analysis of the ways in which the narrative perspectives of the frame narrator and of Mauberley as narrator are blurred, each working to confuse necessary ethical distinctions between art and life, truth and beauty. Yet, in " 'The Perfect Voice': Mauberley as Narrator in Timothy Findley's *Famous Last Words*," Shields sees the narrative blurring between Findley and Mauberley in a more positive light, with Mauberley becoming "Findley's alter ego" (91), personalizing "the perspective" (88), and reinforcing "the fictionality of the authorial voice and its supposed objectivity and omniscience" (97). This kind of disagreement is not easily resolved.

Critics who rely on Findley's own pronouncements about his concerns and aims, and critics who situate their readings in a belief that postmodernist techniques function to question and subvert established power structures, tend to agree with Shields and praise *Famous Last Words*. Williams, situating his reading in a different critical tradition and unwilling to accept postmodernism's claims for itself, advances a fresh perspective on this much-discussed novel by returning to earlier traditions of literary critique. His line of argument seems to be accepted in Martin Kuester's more exclusively formalist reading of the novel in *Framing Truths: Parodic Structures in Contemporary English-Canadian Historical Novels* (1992). Both Williams and Kuester argue that Findley is more properly understood as a modernist, rather than a postmodernist, writer. Kuester argues that *Famous Last Words* is "the ultimate example of parody as a re-functioning of textual models" but that its use of parodic structures is "primarily monologic" (93, 94).

Richard Dellamora takes a different tack, one that I find ultimately more persuasive, in "Becoming-Homosexual/Becoming-Canadian: Ironic Voice and the Politics of Location in Timothy Findley's

Famous Last Words." Dellamora explores what he terms Findley's risk-taking in enunciating the contradictory desires of the homosexual and the Canadian as marginalized figures in relation to Anglo-American high culture and fascist ideology (174). These risks enable Findley to open "new possibilities for writing both as a gay and a Canadian" (173). The ambiguities that Williams reads as complicit Dellamora reads as deeply ironic. Each agrees, however, that the novel questions liberal humanism. For Williams, this questioning marks Findley's betrayal of a moral tradition; for Dellamora, it marks Findley's attempt to create a new morality that can accommodate his own difference as a Canadian homosexual.

Each of these readings provides valuable correctives to earlier blind spots, introducing new contexts of relevance that inevitably change how we understand and value Findley's vision in the novel. In what follows, I draw on these earlier readings while producing a record of my own interactions with this endlessly fascinating text. In a sense, literary criticism always puts the text on trial. Every novel is like someone's "famous last words." As critics, we ask ourselves a series of questions: Is it a testament that will survive? Does it deserve to survive? How do we know? *Famous Last Words* makes this process explicit and asks for our compassion as well as moral and intellectual engagement. I see *Famous Last Words* involving us in a process of remembering history through fiction in order to avoid repeating it in actuality, in what we think of as "the real world." This remembering involves us in the act of refiguring, in the double sense of figuring things out in a way that makes sense to us and of finding images (or figures) in the text that encapsulate those meanings.

Reading of the Text

"FAMOUS LAST WORDS"

Famous last words. What an extraordinary expression. And how mysterious, when looked at closely. Whose words? Why famous? Why last? Within the context of a trial, famous last words might be expected to follow a negative judgement and precede an execution. But this is also an expression that has entered everyday speech. We have all probably used it at one time or another, usually to recognize that, though we have just asserted something with confidence, that assertion may come back to haunt us later. We may have to change our minds, eat our words. English is full of such graphic metaphors. Findley's title draws our attention to language, then, but also to tone. It suggests finality, certainty, and uncertainty, all at the same time. There is always a kind of bravado in the idea of famous last words, a self-conscious self-mocking awareness of the theatricality of the concept, which balances the underlying urgency of the need to communicate one last time before extinction against the awareness that, within a cosmic context, such self-importance may appear slightly ridiculous. Findley takes such risks by continually balancing nostalgia against irony, high moral seriousness against black humour, camp, kitsch, and parody.

One of the recurring words in Findley's writing, a word that gains resonance through its repetition, is "forever." It suggests both eternity, the endless expanse of time, and finality, the end, the last of something. *Famous Last Words* has the same quality of evoking both death and survival. Findley ends the first chapter of *Inside Memory: Pages from a Writer's Workbook* with the idea that "Remembrance is more than honouring the dead. Remembrance is joining them — being one with them in memory. Memory is survival" (7). In *Famous Last Words*, he remembers an ugly period in our recent past: the

Second World War and the attraction that fascism held for many of Europe's intellectual, artistic, and political élite. In his words, "*Famous Last Words* is a novel about what appeared to be — and, indeed, may well have been — the final hours of Western Civilization" (*Inside Memory* 316). Elsewhere, I argue that Findley, like so many other writers of his generation, writes from a perception of humanity irrevocably shaped by the impact of the Holocaust and the dropping of the atomic bombs on Nagasaki and Hiroshima (584). He believes that, through these events, "Our moral concept of horror was altered forever" ("Long Live the Dead" 88). This alteration is responsible for the apocalyptic sense that Western civilization has reached its end.

Appropriately for such a topic, the book contains a large cast of characters involved in a complicated web of plots, all of which concern contested issues of power, authority, and commitment in different arenas of human experience. Innumerable deaths, most of them violent, result from these contestations. The lives and deaths of the thirty or so central characters are linked through the voice and figure of Hugh Selwyn Mauberley, a fictional character that Findley borrowed from Ezra Pound's canonical high-modernist poem *Hugh Selwyn Mauberley*, first published in 1920. These intertextual echoes reinforce Findley's questioning of high modernism's complicity with the fascist right in shaping "the final hours of Western Civilization" into the nightmares of Dachau and Hiroshima. The Holocaust and the atomic bomb, symbolized by these places where unimaginable horrors took human form, became the legacy of his generation.

Famous Last Words has most frequently been discussed in the moral terms outlined above or in formalist terms, as an example of what Linda Hutcheon calls "historiographic metafiction," that is, as self-conscious writing that stresses the similarities between history and fiction as human constructions created through written words. These two perspectives, the moral and the formalist, are not necessarily incompatible, but they do represent different ways of conceptualizing the issues raised in this novel. While "famous last words" record the public version of events that survive as history, in Findley's text they also stand as the private testaments of resistant individuals, accounts that get erased from the official record but that may be imaginatively reconstructed in a fiction truer to our sense of what has happened than the authorized version. In *Famous Last Words*, such an account appears most memorably in Mauberley's final testament, inscribed on the walls of the Grand Elysium Hotel, a testament that provides much of the narration of the novel. But other "last words" prove equally important: Mauberley's father's words before he leaps to his death from the roof of the Arlington Hotel in Boston; Pound's words in "Hugh Selwyn Mauberley," invoked as epigraphs to several of the novel's eight sections and echoed throughout; Lorenzo de Broca's graffiti in the sky; the imprint of a human hand in the caves at Altamira; Luis Quintana's message smuggled out of Spain by Isabella Loverso; Schubert's *Piano Sonata in B Flat Major*, the record that Mauberley plays as he writes, which Freyberg breaks in two and Quinn retrieves as a memento mori (289) — a reminder of mortality. Each draws our attention to the urgent human need to communicate, to remember, and to survive beyond physical death into the memory of future generations.

All these conflicting "famous last words" are contained in Findley's text, which presents its own final words in the full knowledge that they, in turn, will generate more words. This is a novel of endings that hopes to spark fresh beginnings. The title puts the emphasis on words themselves, on imagination, creation, and interpretation as activities that affirm life in the threatening face of destruction. Words are the true heroes of *Famous Last Words*: in it, every human is necessarily flawed, but human values may prevail through attention to the language in which they take shape. Writing is on trial here, but Findley has weighted the scales in its favour. If anything can take us beyond the horror, can tell us what could not be told and still hold out hope for a better world, then, says *Famous Last Words*, it is writing.

HUGH SELWYN MAUBERLEY: "A COMPULSIVE WITNESS"

Mauberley is on trial, but he is also the chief witness, for both the defence and the prosecution. His words are his life. Writing in *Inside Memory*, Findley links his obsession with words to his own and Mauberley's vocation as writers. He claims:

Words are my safety deposit boxes — my guarantees against the extortion of what I know. Words are the only currency I have,

26

and without them, I might as well fill my mind with stones and swim out to sea. *I am a writer, and a writer writes* — Mauberley's creed. (190–91)

The slippage from his own need for words to Mauberley's suggests the importance of Mauberley in the overall design of this novel about words and their impact on the world. Although there are many possible approaches that we might take in entering into the experience of this novel, this section begins with the character of Mauberley himself.

Like Rushdie, Mauberley is a writer whose life and words have become inseparable. In chapter 1, he is stalked by enemies who wish to kill not only him but "his words as well." He writes because he cannot do otherwise: he is "a compulsive witness." What he writes is feared for the evidence that it provides of the guilts and complicities of the powerful. His notebooks are described in a haunting metaphor as being "feared like a morgue where the dead are kept on ice — with all their incriminating wounds intact" (21). The metaphor of the morgue becomes literal in chapter 2, in which the American soldier Annie Oakley is described as "the Keeper of the Morgue" because he guards the corpses piled in the saloon of the Grand Elysium Hotel (57). This metaphor (in which notebooks, hotel, and novel each become a kind of morgue) reminds us of the human cost of war. Although war deaths are usually perceived differently than murders, Findley's reference to "incriminating wounds" implies that war deaths are also murders. Indeed, "incriminating" suggests that someone must take responsibility for all the war dead, not just those murdered in the concentration camps but also the soldiers killed in battle and the civilians who got in the way. Mauberley's words, like Findley's novel, act as "incriminating wounds": they accuse. And they deny the excuse of those who would say, as many did at Nuremberg (the setting for the Second World War's most famous trials), "*I did not know* . . ." (9). Mauberley's witnessing shows that they *did* know and ensures that we know too. His refusal to accept others' alibis makes him unpopular with everyone. As Pound puts it in the novel, he has made himself an "arse-eyed traitor to the whole world!" (7). Mauberley as writer, witness, and traitor provides the focus for Findley's exploration of the relations between art and politics, narrative and responsibility, and history and myth.

But Mauberley also serves a more immediately practical function. His life and his words are the thread that links the many different geographical settings of the novel, mostly in Europe, and the two dominant time periods of the novel: that of Mauberley's record (spanning roughly 1936–43) and that of the reception of his record in May 1945. The bulk of the novel (from chapter 3 through 8) either reinscribes Mauberley's words or records the debates that they engender among the men who first find them. The prologue and chapters 1 and 2 are narrated by an omniscient narrator who appears to sympathize with Mauberley's fate to the point of blurring narrative perspective in key places.

The novel opens with a two-page prologue, set in 1910, when Mauberley is twelve. After a brief conversation on the roof of the Arlington Hotel in Boston, where Mauberley was born, his father leaps "fifteen stories to his death," leaving his son a silver pencil and a cryptic message: " 'He who jumps to his death has cause,' it said. 'He who leaps has purpose. Always remember: I leapt' " (2). This opening vignette establishes the pattern for the action that follows. Symbolically, it shows us a traumatic moment of choice witnessed by Mauberley, a helpless but heavily implicated bystander: a father's suicide, a son's abandonment. The conversation preceding the suicide rehearses many of the obsessions developed in the novel: a love that turns to stone, our failure to be whole, our need to communicate, our deafness to words that we do not want to hear, the view from above, and the view from below. His father's message introduces a philosophical debate about human agency, seen as a choice between notions of fate and free will. The text eventually shows that Mauberley's father conceptualizes this debate far too simplistically.

The scene revolves around questions of responsibility. Mauberley's father insists that no one is to blame for his situation, yet his response must be to choose his death. Nonetheless, he leaves more questions than answers behind. He appears to be the voice of conscience that his age refused to hear, yet his suicide abandons his son to the very world that he himself can no longer bear. And surely that is unconscionable. Hints in this scene and throughout the book imply that Mauberley's mother has previously abandoned both of them. Although his father states that he does not blame her, it is clear that he does blame her for "her failure to be whole" (2), a blame that the frame narrator appears to endorse.

What are the implications of this scene for understanding the rest of the novel? It provides a plausible psychological explanation for Mauberley's future actions. He is the product of a broken home. It establishes the pattern of his life: he becomes a compulsive witness to history, registering the impact of events that he has taken little part in initiating. His guilt over his inability to intervene and save his father colours his future relationships, dooming them to failure. This scene establishes him as a vulnerable person, no doubt traumatized by this personal tragedy, with whom we can sympathize. But it also makes him a symbolic figure, representative of an orphaned generation cut adrift by the abdication of authority of its parent generation. He becomes a member of the generation following the First World War (in the 1920s) called "the lost generation." This interplay between private emotion and public significance characterizes Findley's use of Mauberley throughout the novel.

The distinction that Mauberley's father makes between cause and purpose embodies the enabling American myth of individual endeavour as the sole distinguishing mark between those who succeed and those who fail. As he puts it, those who have "cause" succumb passively to fate. They react. They are losers. They do not initiate action; they act "because" of some external prompt. They are, perhaps, like Mauberley's mother, who cannot help being herself. Those who have "purpose," on the other hand, believe that they have choice, that they have chosen their respective fate, even in suicide. In refusing to abandon their claim to agency, they show strength even in their choice of death. This ideology is often celebrated in literature and criticism as the American dream, the enabling myth of American success.

In *Famous Last Words*, Findley shows how close this individualist dream comes to the fascist ideology of "the 'new man,' the élite of heroic supermen, '*artist*-tyrants' " (Hamilton xxii), which motivated Hitler and Mussolini in the formation of their regimes, usually characterized as the opposite of the democratic ideals motivating the Allies who opposed and eventually defeated them in the Second World War. (In the novel, Findley tends to equate Fascist and Nazi ideologies, and I follow his example in my commentary throughout.) It is a short step from separating the losers, who jump with cause, from the élite, who leap with purpose, to the Nietzschean notion of supermen and racial purity that inspired the Nazis in their genocidal campaigns against Jews, Gypsies, communists, the mentally unfit, and homosexuals. Fascism creates victims and then blames them for their misfortune. So, far too often, does capitalism.

The novel as a whole can be seen as a gloss on this first misguided suicide, in which Mauberley's father sets a pattern of abdication as heroic failure, of turning his back on "the world [that] is too much with us" (1). Mauberley himself eventually conforms to this pattern, fleeing the war and awaiting inevitable murder in another hotel half a world away. This pattern links this American father and son to the Duke of Windsor, who abandoned throne and country for the American divorcée Wallis Simpson. After his abdication, he spent the rest of his life in exile, usually in hotels. The idea of abdication becomes central in *Famous Last Words*. The Duke and Duchess of Windsor tried to make the abdication a popular symbol of romance, of the heart triumphing over the head, but many continued to see this act as a serious dereliction of duty and a betrayal of the responsibilities that the duke had when he was king.

Findley exploits this moral ambiguity in *Famous Last Words* in order to ask how we interpret such key moments in history, which seem to be summed up in dramatic but ambiguous gestures such as the abdication. He asks us to consider what abdication as a concept really means. In the royal-abdication story, the duke leaves his responsibilities as king for a woman of dubious character and a transient life in hotels. The hotel becomes a powerful symbol of rootlessness and self-indulgence, and Findley exploits it in the scenes of Mauberley's father's death and of Mauberley's murder. These hotels, temporary abodes for a permanently unhoused imagination, suggest the alienated sensibility of twentieth-century life as well as the failure of these characters to make meaningful lives, rooted in commitment to a particular community.

This juxtaposition of father and son as representatives of the dereliction of duty predominant in the age explains why chapter 1 leaps forward to March 1945, when Mauberley is forty-seven, taking leave of his surrogate father, the American poet Ezra Pound, and heading in flight from his enemies toward the Grand Elysium Hotel and his own death two months later. The deaths of father and son are juxtaposed because they are related, part of a larger pattern that Findley tries to convey. In fact, the novel is full of death-bed scenes of every kind, usually staged far from the traditional bed. Each

Mauberley seeks a height before meeting the death that he has chosen. The novel then becomes a kind of postmortem inquiry into the deaths of both men and the related deaths of their different worlds: the pre-First World War era of the father, and the Second World War period of the son.

The novel first depicts Mauberley at these two moments — at ages twelve and forty-seven. In the first instance, he witnesses a singular death. In the second, he flees amid mass destruction to save his own life. Each scene is told from the point of view of an omniscient third-person narrator, usually called the frame narrator in Findley criticism. This narrator announces Mauberley's death at the beginning of chapter 2, May 1945: "Mauberley was found by strangers" (37). There is no suspense about his end. The suspense lies entirely in how he got there. To be found by strangers is a sad and lonely fate, yet appropriate given the life that he has led. First Mauberley's body is discovered, clutching the silver pencil, his father's legacy, and then his words, adorning the walls and ceilings of four rooms.

It is not until chapter 3 that we begin to read Mauberley's account of events. We read along with Quinn, the demolitions expert on the Allied team cleaning up at the end of the war, who has been assigned to assess this new evidence. Even here, Quinn chooses to begin reading in the middle of the story rather than "where Mauberley himself had obviously intended" his readers to begin (59). Mauberley had initiated his story with an apocalyptically prophetic epigraph from the book of Daniel. This epigraph stresses the certainty of divine judgement. But Quinn chooses to begin reading beneath a second epigraph, which has been "scrawled outside the disciplined alignment of the others," an epigraph that runs: *"All I have written here is true; except the lies"* (59). This marginal epigraph casts the certainties of the first one into doubt, stressing the uncertainties of human understanding and the difficulty of separating truth from lies.

With this ambiguous warning echoing in our minds, we find ourselves reading Mauberley's mythologizing of the Duke and Duchess of Windsor's arrival in Dubrovnik, 17 August 1936 (60), followed by Quinn's shocked response as he stops to analyse what he has just read. The rest of the novel then moves back and forth between the more distant history recreated through Mauberley's writing on the wall and the more recent history in which Quinn

31

absorbs and responds to Mauberley's version of events, debating his reaction to them with his fellow officer Freyberg. Progress through the embedded narrative inscribed by Mauberley now becomes linear, and time in Quinn's period continues to move forward sequentially. Our reading of the walls along with Quinn in the rest of chapter 3 moves from entries labelled "China: August, 1924" (66), through "Rapallo: March 7th, 1936" (77), "Venice: May 5th, 1936" (84), "The *Nahlin*: August, 1936" (94), "Paris: September, 1936" (106), "*Nauly*: September, 1936" (108), to "Paris: December, 1936" (121). Places and dates suggest a factual orientation that helps us to locate ourselves in space and time.

Chapter 4 covers from 1937 to 1940 in Spain and Portugal, with a brief interlude in Berlin. Chapter 5 deals only with 1940, moving between the Nazis in Berlin, the Windsors on the ship sailing toward the Bahamas, and Mauberley in Italy, where he learns of Isabella Loverso's murder. Chapter 6 recounts a single episode on 4 July 1941, "*The Spitfire Bazaar*" in Nassau (265), marked by the skywriting of the young antifascist Italian poet Lorenzo de Broca. Chapter 7 introduces a further intrusion of the omniscient narrator, who recounts Estrade's arrival at the hotel when Mauberley is still alive, and Rudecki's discovery of her in May 1945. This chapter takes Mauberley's narrative from 1941 into 1942 and covers events in Germany and England. Chapter 8, the final chapter, carries his narrative to its apparent conclusion, recounting the murder of Sir Harry Oakes in Nassau in 1943 and its aftermath.

The entry in this chapter entitled "April, 1945" (384–89) recounts Mauberley's death as he might have experienced it, apparently from the point of view of the omniscient narrator who begins the book. But such an assumption is cast into doubt by the entry that follows this sequence: "Quinn finished reading at dawn" (389). This entry seems to imply that Quinn has just read the preceding one, either on the walls (which would mean that Mauberley wrote himself a death scene) or in his own mind, having entered the story so fully that he has continued on from where it ends.

The novel concludes with Mauberley's "epilogue," a metaphorical parable about how we make meanings and understand events, about how reason always seems accompanied by unreason, about light and darkness, hope and despair, good and evil — all in all, a chilling reminder that what we most fear and unconsciously repress still lies in wait for our civilization. Quinn takes a final look at these words, which he knows will be destroyed, and adds his own notation: "*May, 1945*" (396). He makes a gesture that is apparently futile but none- theless necessary from his point of view. He also needs to claim his place in history by making and leaving his mark. This act links him to Mauberley. Through reading Mauberley's story, Quinn relives it in his mind. Mauberley's words have turned Quinn into yet another compulsive witness to history, who, in his turn, is accused by his companion, Freyberg, of acting the traitor. Findley's work is full of such repetitions. Here, they show the importance that he places on historical witnessing, on scenes of reading, and on the human act of interpretation and judgement.

It is important to remember that, while Findley endorses the *act* of witnessing, he does not excuse the complicity of the witness who should have intervened instead of merely watching, nor does he necessarily approve of *what* Mauberley witnesses. Mauberley shows us his version of history, but he also reveals many sides of himself. The side that dominates the novel is that of compulsive witness, but he also reveals himself to be an élitist aesthete, a coward, a Fascist sympathizer, a masochist, a commissioner of murders if not literally a murderer himself, and a traitor to many of his friends and beliefs.

Readers of realist fiction have become accustomed to central char- acters that they can admire, especially when these characters employ the first person, a narrative voice that tends to draw the reader into complicity with the speaker. Findley implies that he identifies with Quinn's imaginative solidarity with Mauberley by having Quinn wear Mauberley's scarf (394) and by wearing a similar scarf in interviews about the book ("initialled 'H.S.M.' for Hugh Selwyn Mauberley," Bruce Meyer and Brian O'Riordan point out in their interview with Findley ["Timothy Findley" 45]). Yet Findley mani- pulates these conventions ultimately to question them in *Famous Last Words*. He shows how our understanding of events is con- structed through such narrative devices. We are not allowed to identify fully with Mauberley, to admire him, or to reject him completely. Instead, he is a figure who forces us to confront the moral dilemmas posed by fascism through remembering what war propa- ganda has encouraged us to forget: the fascination that fascism held for many Western intellectuals before and even during the Second World War. The book balances our knowledge of how Nazis and

Fascists have been demonized in the years since that war against the narrative of fascination and complicity that Mauberley tells.

Mauberley is the focus of the novel's explorations, but in my view, he is not the hero of the text. In making this assessment, I am disagreeing not only with reviewers such as Donald Hair, who argues that Mauberley is "the artist-hero or writer-hero" (12), but also with Findley himself, who, in defining a hero as "someone who must do what he must do despite the consequences," sees Mauberley as a hero "because in writing what he does on the walls he must condemn himself and everything he stood for" ("Timothy Findley" 49). To Findley, Mauberley succumbs to the worst within himself in yielding to the attractions of fascism, but he redeems himself in the end by turning away from its lies, feeling an even greater "responsibility to the truth" (50). But that is not quite what happens in the novel. Findley's comment starkly opposes lies and truth, but in the novel they are more closely intertwined. All Mauberley's "truths" are presented in a fictional format and contextualized by an epigraph that makes it almost impossible to tell fact from fiction.

To my mind, Findley's comments in this interview privilege one moment in Mauberley's life, and one of many conflicting urges within him, in a way that oversimplifies the complexities of the book and even contradicts some of its insights. His comments imply that the writer can function independently of his society and that his art can transcend the pressures of his times, yet *Famous Last Words* debunks these modernist myths and even reveals how they became complicit with fascism, obscuring the material and historical realities that they pretend to illuminate. The novel shows artists who are complicit with fascism and artists who defy it, but it always shows their writing as part of conflicts within larger systems of signification. It is unclear in the interview whether Findley is opposing truth-telling and artistry or whether he is conflating them. Given the form of Mauberley's truth in the text, he seems to be conflating them. The misguided élitism that would excuse Mauberley's fascism on the basis of his artistry has guided modernist aesthetics and literary criticism until very recently. Now that kind of thinking is being questioned. A writer's politics inevitably affects his/her artistic vision and achievement.

We will see later how Mauberley's fascism infects his narrative and how Findley's sympathy for Mauberley as an artist-hero introduces problematic elements into the frame narrator's omniscient narration. For the moment, we need only note that Findley's definition of a hero could also be applied to Hitler. As Alfred Kazin notes, "Mussolini and Hitler described themselves as artists who performed on history; the masses were their raw material" (27). Daniel Pearlman quotes Hyam Maccoby on the intimate relationship between aestheticism and the rise of fascism, noting that "The aesthetes could view 'Hitler as the Artist in Power, a grotesque caricature of Shelley's "unacknowledged legislators of the world," ' for it was axiomatic with them to subordinate the sphere of morality to the sphere of art" (112). It is one thing to reproduce such thinking as part of Mauberley's worldview; it is another to endorse it when history has revealed its deep flaws as a justifying ideology. In my view, *Famous Last Words* does not elevate the heroism of the individual artist above questions of morality. If there is a hero in this text, it is the reader, who must wrestle with the intractable questions that it poses. Art provides no special salvation. The artist is not always a hero. Our survival depends on the engagement of the entire community in the process of making meanings from the materials of life and art as we encounter them. We cannot exempt the artist or his/her work from the trial of history, but we can do our best to ensure that it is a fair trial.

SCENES OF READING

Famous Last Words asks us to consider not only how we read but also why we read. And, especially, why we read fiction. Why, fifty years later, should we care whether or not the Duchess of Windsor collaborated with the Nazis, whether Ezra Pound's fascism affected his poetry, or who murdered Sir Harry Oakes? My discussion of the book's initial reception, especially in Britain, demonstrates that these questions are still compelling for a variety of reasons. Motivation may include curiosity about the lives of the rich and famous and speculative delight in the possibility of uncovering hidden scandals. Findley's text plays to these voyeuristic motives, embellishing hints in the historical narratives into shocking scenes in the private lives of these famous people. But their lives are not evoked for these reasons only. They become symbols of the debates of their period, and their lives illustrate problems that we are still struggling to resolve. Furthermore, it still seems important to try to establish what really happened and why. Many contradictory versions have been offered, some records appear to have been suppressed, and new information is still being discovered. These scenes of reading are where evidence is sifted, weighed, dismissed, or admitted before final judgements can be made in the trial of history.

The next section will deal with historical substance and fabrications in *Famous Last Words*. This section considers the ways in which the novel stages its own scenes of reading and interpretation in order to guide reader response and to help in the formation of judgements. We have seen how the prologue and first chapter introduce Mauberley as an abandoned son, compulsive witness, and fleeing traitor. Chapter 2 introduces the men who find his body and see the story that he has inscribed from his notebooks onto the walls of the hotel. They function metaphorically as judge and jury, though two of these men — Quinn and Freyberg — quickly assume the roles of defence and opposition lawyers. They are the first readers of Mauberley's masterpiece and the first to put his writing on trial. (His earlier writings, of course, have been tried and found wanting by the journalist Julia Franklin, but we learn this later.)

Mauberley's Testament

Each of these American Allied soldiers who finds Mauberley's testament shares certain character traits, and not others, with Mauberley. These similarities and differences place his character in sharper perspective. They also reveal how much each reader brings of his own preconceptions to his reading of the text. Like Mauberley, Freyberg is a compulsive witness, but he compiles his dossiers, lists, and elaborate filing systems in order not to explain or excuse but to condemn the atrocities of the Nazis. He becomes Mauberley's accuser. Like Mauberley, Quinn is an aesthete, someone who loves beauty, art, literature, and music, and a compulsive hero-worshipper who lets his feelings interfere with his judgement. He becomes Mauberley's advocate. Like Mauberley, Oakley is easily blinded by glamour and material possessions. He steals the silver pencil that was Mauberley's gift from his father, appropriating the symbol of Mauberley's heritage without understanding its significance. Yet his nickname hints at a gender ambiguity that also links him to Mauberley. Like Mauberley, Rudecki reveres celebrity and fears for his masculinity. He sees Mauberley's words as spectacle, nothing more. The response of each of these men to Mauberley's words is partial. Initially, the writing on the walls seems "'alarming' (to Quinn), 'damning' (to Freyberg) and 'fuckin' fantastic' (to Rudecki)" (57). Oakley is not even interested. It remains for each of us as readers to create a reading that can account for all these responses rather than choosing one from among them.

The substantive philosophical debates occur between Freyberg and Quinn, yet the context of reception that the other men create is crucial. For them, style has replaced substance as the guarantor of meaning, and Hollywood films have replaced books as cultural icons. For Oakley, movies are more real than the life that he is living. He sees through the glamorized filters of the Hollywood movie *Casablanca*. Mauberley becomes more real to Rudecki when he learns that this badly dressed corpse is a man once considered important. But neither of these men is curious enough to probe more deeply. This willingness to forget, and this lack of curiosity about the past, defines the attitude that *Famous Last Words* seeks to contest. It suggests that the passion that both Freyberg and Quinn bring to the problem of Mauberley is preferable to such indifference.

Both men care about justice. But Freyberg responds to the injustice of Dachau by embracing vengeance, whereas Quinn chooses puzzlement, shock, and pity. The arguments between these men dramatize the central problems of our time. After Dachau, how do we define civilization? After such horror, how can one write? What does justice mean? How can it be achieved in an unjust world? Can writers be held responsible for the impact of their words? Can we separate the political actions of a writer such as Pound (or the fictional Mauberley) from his art? What is the difference between an artist and a con artist? How do we oppose evil without falling into the trap of demonizing the enemy? How do we respond to hatred without accepting its terms of reference and allowing it to continue unchecked? How can we successfully oppose violence in a nonviolent way? These are perennial questions. They are not easily answered but they must be continually reposed and recontextualized.

One of the contexts that Findley questions through Quinn is the oppositional mentality of "us versus them." Fascist ideology was built on this opposition. So is the Penelope cabal within the text. The nationalist states in Nazi Germany and Fascist Italy created a sense of solidarity through their opposition to external enemies who resisted their expansion and to internal enemies identified as Jews, Gypsies, homosexuals, and communists. As Burton Hatlen puts it, "fascism finds its logical fulfillment in a militarism directed against the enemy without and an anti-semitism which seeks to destroy the enemy within" (151). The Allies, in fighting these states, adopted a similar mode of oppositional thinking. They did not glorify militarism or spread anti-Semitic hatred, but they did demonize their Nazi and Fascist enemies. Quinn, we are told, resists such Allied propaganda. He is "paranoid" about words such as " 'We' and 'they' " (47). These words oversimplify complex problems without explaining them. To demonize the enemy is to refuse to understand not only him but also whatever part of ourselves is susceptible to such corruption.

In "The Nazi Myth," Philippe Lacoue-Labarthe and Jean-Luc Nancy argue that Nazism was too fundamentally a culmination of Western culture to dismiss as a mere aberration. Although it "does not sum up the West, nor represent its necessary finality," Nazism should not be seen as "a dossier of simple accusation, but rather as one element in a general deconstruction of the history in which our own provenance lies" (312). Freyberg too quickly takes refuge in compiling such "a dossier of simple accusation." Quinn, on the other hand, falls into an error at the opposite extreme: he begins to worship Mauberley, eerily echoing Mauberley's own worship of the Duke of Windsor when he was Prince of Wales and then King Edward VIII, of Wallis Simpson, and of Harry Reinhardt, and Pound's of Mussolini. The aesthete's worship for the strong ruler and the powerful personality contributed another element to the success of the Nazis. Quinn and Freyberg see the dangers in each other's thinking, but not in their own. Findley puts us in a position in which we can see more clearly, in which we can begin to participate in the kind of "general deconstruction" of our history for which Lacoue-Labarthe and Nancy call.

Quinn seems right in suggesting that the implications of Freyberg's thinking are dangerous. To imply that Mauberley's murder is "understandable, and the method excusable" (49), denies the primacy of the rule of law, even in wartime, and leads logically to the kinds of breakdown experienced in the former Yugoslavia throughout 1993. Yet Freyberg is also right in challenging Quinn's naïveté on several occasions, for Dachau has changed the context in which events can be read. Freyberg expresses Findley's view when he tells Quinn: "you think of insanity as being the exclusive property of madmen. *Which it ain't*" (50). Without wishing to glorify irrationality and atavistic impulses as Fascism did, Freyberg sees that the old humanistic faith in the power of reason is stymied by the phenomenon of the Nazi torturer who can kill by day and enjoy classical music in the evening. Freyberg's understanding that history is already being rewritten to exonerate the Nazis is also crucial to grasping Findley's subject in *Famous Last Words*. Quinn assumes that Mauberley's record can be taken at face value as *"evidence"* (52), but Freyberg makes Findley's point that evidence itself is a human construction and therefore suspect in an era of propaganda and illusion (53). If Freyberg is the ultimate resistant reader, suspicious of everything, then Quinn is too willing to surrender himself to the sweep of the narrative, convinced in advance that "he would exonerate Hugh Selwyn Mauberley" (58). With the strengths and weaknesses of these two positions dramatized for us, we are encouraged to identify with neither.

The final exchange between the two men encapsulates what has happened in the public world of the text. The Cold War is about to begin, and history is being rewritten once again to accommodate a change of enemies: "Nazis are out. And Commies are in" (392). Freyberg strikes Quinn in the stomach and then denies responsibility. "The wind did it," he says (393). Throughout the text, Quinn has looked for art, beauty, and evidence of human survival in the face of extinction, while Freyberg has been obsessed with the abuse of power. Findley cares about both, especially about how they are connected. Freyberg's gesture seems to argue that, whatever our experience, the ability to assign meaning to events rests with the powerful. His resistance to official manipulations of the representation of reality is located in his "Dachau Collection" (393). The photographs, like the punch, remind him of a violence that cannot be explained away. Quinn keeps different mementoes: Mauberley's scarf and "the two dusty halves of the Alfred Cortot recording of the Schubert Sonata" (394). One chooses to focus on the horror of the death camps, the other on nostalgia for the lost humanity and order of classical art. We cannot choose between these two men and their souvenirs of war without denying what we most need to understand: how such horror and such beauty could coexist under Fascism. Neither man has all the answers. But each is committed to human decency, and each chooses his own way of remembering how easy it has been for human beings to lose sight of that value. Each provides us with a place to begin, but no answers. If we are to survive the public deceptions of our own times, Findley implies, then we will need both Quinn's trust and Freyberg's suspiciousness. Both hope and despair mark the idealism essential to human survival.

"The Caves of Altamira"

A central incident in Mauberley's narrative is the search for shelter that he made with Isabella Loverso in the caves at Altamira during an aerial bombardment. As so often in this book, Findley juxtaposes a horror without and a beauty within. A man who worships the past, Mauberley characterizes Altamira as "the furthest past of all" (158–59). It proves a haven not only from the war but also from the present. Later, he reproduces the ancient paintings of the caves on the ceiling of the second room where his words cover the walls (51). In those caves, he thinks, "the painted walls reverberate with the cries of Ice Age animals and men that have been dead two hundred thousand years and more" (159). It is this kind of immortality that he seeks for his own words. Mauberley reads the pictographs as an expression of the human will to survive and to claim an identity, translating the images of stars and bisons into words:

> *This is my mark; it said. My mark that I was here. All I can tell you of my self and of my time and of the world in which I lived is in this signature: this hand print; mine.*
> *I saw these animals. I saw this grass. I saw these stars. We made these wars. And then the ice came.* (173)

Mauberley concludes his analysis with the conviction: "And I knew I was sitting at the heart of the human race — which is its will to say *I am*" (173). Findley sees Mauberley beginning to turn away from fascism as a result of this imaginative insight and toward a creative instinct that links all human beings ("My Final Hour" 15). But faith in the imagination and its creative expression can easily be distorted if confined to an artistic élite. The Altamira caves meant a great deal to modernist poets seeking, as Hugh Kenner puts it, " 'the new, the really new,' which should be fit company for an Altamira bison[;] these had been the intentions of their vortex, dragging a dark world up into the light, forging an ecumenical reality where all times could meet without the romance of time . . ." (qtd. in Kazin 32). Throughout *Famous Last Words*, Findley draws on this imagery of dark and light and on an eternal art that transcends the temporal. But such a mythologizing of the past as a source of primal power can easily be twisted to deny the affirmation that Findley celebrates in these passages by asserting, instead, an individual will to power that despises the human race. That seems to be what happened under Fascism.

The next scene shows Mauberley confronted with the realization that he has betrayed his better self by placing his assertion, *"I am,"* within the context of the Penelope conspiracy and fascist politics rather than in solidarity with more humane values. Lorenzo de Broca, the young antifascist poet, accuses him of betraying "the good and genius" that he had seen in him and asks: "why have you left from us? Why have you gone away from your self?" (175). Although shaken by what he concedes is the truth, Mauberley remains committed to the lie at this point in his story. He records how he deliberately turned from a search for truth to embrace a web of lies, adopting, with the Duke and Duchess of Windsor and their fascist friends, the cynical motto *"the truth is in our hands now"* (177). Their egotism expressed a will to power that denied community with the cave dwellers, who longed to survive extinction by leaving some mark of achievement in accord with the truth of their communal experience. Hannah Arendt describes how the élite of this period in Europe subscribed to a

demoralizing fascination in the possibility that gigantic lies and monstrous falsehood can eventually be established as unquestioned facts, that man may be free to change his own past at will, and that the difference between truth and falsehood may cease to be objective and become a mere matter of power and cleverness, of pressure and infinite repetition. (qtd. in Surette 340–41)

Mauberley's betrayal stands for those of the élite of his generation. The question for us is whether or not his writing on the wall is part of that gigantic con job (as Freyberg believes) or an attempt to expose and disown it (as Quinn hopes). The omniscient narrator weighs the scales in Quinn's favour. He shows Mauberley reaching the end of his story, asking himself, "Had all the truths been told?" (385). He reveals that Mauberley chose to locate his record in Isabella's rooms because she

> had believed above all other things in the value of the human mind. And she had placed her faith in the currency of the human mind, the written word. Her husband had died for the written word, and her children because of it. . . . [S]he had remained determined to salvage what she could of words and hold them up against the sword. (385)

Like Isabella, Mauberley holds his words against the ice pick that Reinhardt wields. And Findley holds his words against violence everywhere.

Faced with a choice between the cynicism of the fascists and the idealism of Isabella, Mauberley appears to return to the antifascist ranks in the end. Although they do not employ written words, the cave images seem to be reinterpreted as symbols of the value of the human mind. Certainly, the symbolism of the caves as repro- duced by Mauberley awes and reassures Quinn. At first, he thinks, "Maybe he had needed to create another image of the world: innocent and shining . . ." (76). He sees Mauberley's art as providing an alternative to reality. At this point, he links this image with Wallis Simpson's synthetic dreams of marvellous successes. Later, he sees this dream of perfection in an even more sinister light, remembering Mauberley's mother:

> . . . Quinn looked at the animals over his head — and the moon and the stars and the hand — and he remembered something long forgotten. Mauberley's mother, so the story went, had lost her mind because she was obsessed with perfection she could not achieve as a pianist. That no one could achieve. Just as Freyberg was obsessed with perfections of another kind that no one could achieve. Because — if they could — there would be nothing written on the walls at all. (155–56)

Here writing seems to arise from imperfection, from need, from a gap in understanding and a longing for completion. Quinn sees the artistic impulse as a reaching out for perfections not achievable in the social or political world. Fascism's mistake, he seems to imply, was to try to aestheticize the political. The refusal to compromise with imperfection, when turned inward, leads to madness and misery; when turned outward, it leads to genocide, conspiracy theories, and perpetual warfare. Yet the dream can create great beauty. Can one remain committed to this dream without punishing those (including oneself) who inevitably fail to meet its standards? This is the question that Findley seems to be asking himself and us, his readers.

Without condoning the excesses done in the name of the dream, Quinn wishes to remain true to the dream itself, as he believes that Mauberley was. Lying in bed when he is finished reading Mauberley's "stars" on the walls, "All he could think of was: *they are there. And they will not go out. Like other stars*" (391). He sees art as unchanging, surviving through the centuries and transcending time and nature. But he is wrong. The next day he learns that the walls will be destroyed because their message is uncongenial to the postwar powers. While Mauberley and Quinn read the caves and their reproduced symbolism as a testament to human endurance, Findley encodes that reading within his own contemporary awareness of the fragility of human values and their changing symbolisms. In the atomic age, it is no longer possible to take the continuity of the human race for granted. After the betrayal of the artists, it is no longer possible to assume a transcendent power in art alone.

Mauberley's epilogue implies that the story of *Famous Last Words* is open-ended. A mysterious shape rises from the sea and disappears "before it can be identified" (395), an atavistic reminder of what lies on *"the other side of reason"* (396). Like the hand on the ceiling of the cave and the hotel, this mysterious threat requires acknowledgement, asserting *"I am here. I wait"* (396). Until we deal with both sides of our heritage, Findley implies, we will not be free of the nightmare and the dread. The Nazis showed the dangers of exalting the primitive, but there may be equal dangers in repressing it.

The reproduced cave symbolism from Altamira provides one frame through which Mauberley's narrative can be read, a frame that unites modernism's fascination with the archaic with the symbolic systems of Stone Age peoples in ancient Europe. The epigraph that Mauberley chooses for his narrative, taken from Daniel, suggests another frame: that of divine prophecy and absolute judgement. This epigraph introduces a rhetoric of good and evil into Findley's consideration of the historical phenomena of Nazism and Fascism. Freyberg begins reading it aloud, and Quinn completes the line when Freyberg stops: "IN THE SAME HOUR CAME FORTH FINGERS OF A MAN'S HAND, AND WROTE OVER AGAINST THE CANDLESTICK UPON THE PLAISTER OF THE WALL OF THE KING'S PALACE ...."; *"and the King saw the part of the hand that wrote"* (52).

We are not told what the hand writes. Knowledge of the biblical scene known as Belshazzar's feast is assumed. By placing it at the front of his narrative, Mauberley suggests a parallel between the biblical writing on the wall and his own. Like the message found in Daniel 5.5, his narrative becomes an accusation, not only of himself but also of his generation. The biblical message finally becomes explicit in Mauberley's account of the Spitfire Bazaar. Lorenzo de Broca writes the words in the sky above the bazaar in the Bahamas: *"mene mene tekel upharsin;* the final scrawl, the ultimate graffiti ... *thou art weighed in the balance — and found wanting"* (287). De Broca is repeating his earlier, more personal accusation, directed only to Mauberley (175), and redirecting it, no longer as a question but as a blanket judgement, posed in the absolute authority of biblical language, to Mauberley's entire circle. De Broca's rephrased judgement, "DEATH TO FASCISTS EVERYWHERE" (288), replaces his earlier distress over betrayal with a violent rejection that is itself deeply troubling.

The account of this scene is perplexing. It stretches credibility that Mauberley would bother to devote so much space to recreating this disaster from the point of view of a minor character, the seedy gossip journalist called Little Nell, who dies in a blackly comic accident as he reaches out for Lana Turner's breasts. Yet if we think of the novel as a long deathbed-style confession, then the Little Nell scene can be read as a postmodernist parody of the prolonged sentimentalizing of

Little Nell's death in Dickens's *The Old Curiosity Shop*. Findley is more interested in drawing attention to the construction of his narrative than in adhering to verisimilitude. His Little Nell is an unsavoury character who dies a meaningless and grotesque death. Yet despite the gender-bending parody that this scene provides of Dickens's sentimentality, Findley's writing reproduces that sentimentality in its own black way. In another register, Little Nell and his fantasies about Lana Turner are mirrored by Annie Oakley and his fantasies about her in the frame narrative. Their obsessions with the movie star as the ideal woman seem refractions of Mauberley's obsession with the glamorous Duchess of Windsor. The contrast between their masculinity and their female names highlights Mauberley's own gender confusions. And all these mirrorings draw attention to Findley's controlling hand in the construction of these various fictional realities.

The epigraph to the chapter is taken from Lauro de Bosis, the historical figure on whom Lorenzo de Broca is based. Findley appears to turn de Bosis's insight into the excesses of fascism against itself by depicting his antifascist gesture as one of fascism's dangerous excesses, killing fifty-five innocent people. In this sense, de Broca's airplane is well named after the mythological Icarus, for he also demonstrates a dangerous hubris that leads to a fiery fall. Although York sees de Broca's fall as "noble" in its antifascist intent (*Front Lines* 89), I see Findley looking beyond intent to the effects of the aerial bombardment and the needless deaths that it causes. In this sense, de Broca's fall proves both destructive and self-destructive.

The chapter asks how we can oppose anything without becoming contaminated by that which we oppose. Just as Findley's masculine Little Nell reminds us of his female namesake and her sentimental death, so de Broca seems condemned to repeat the Nazi violence that he opposes. Mauberley even uses "holocaust" to describe the fire that de Broca unleashes (285), apparently accidentally. Quinn, reading of these deaths, mourns those killed indiscriminately. His seems to be the kind of sensibility that Findley wishes to encourage throughout this chapter, a sensibility that remembers the individual humanity and potential of all the war dead, regardless of affiliation. By placing the sign taken from the gate at Dachau at the end of this chapter, Findley juxtaposes its absolute judgement, "ARBEIT MACHT FREI," that is, *"work shall set you free"* (292), against de Broca's, "DEATH TO FASCISTS EVERYWHERE" (288). The juxtaposition implies that they mirror each other in their reduction of humanity to a formula. Only Quinn, the novel implies, sees people as individuals and not as part of some larger group. But his response also seems an insufficient answer to the questions that this chapter raises. Although Quinn mourns what is lost, he seems incapable of moving beyond sympathy into action. If de Broca's opposition to fascism proved self-destructive and self-defeating, what kind of opposition would prove more successful? Quinn's rejection of violence — significantly, he is a demolitions expert — seems insufficient in the face of the violence that Mauberley records.

Variations on Pound

Quinn feels the same sympathy for Ezra Pound, the American poet who broadcast hate-filled messages in favour of the Fascists during the war, as he does for the innocent victims of the Spitfire Bazaar. The act of caging Pound after his capture, like de Broca's fiery massacre, shows fascist excesses infecting their opponents. The novelist has little need of invention when history supplies such material. Yet the American military's caging of Pound, and his subsequent incarceration in a facility for the mentally ill, had no effect on his literary reputation. He was canonized in the universities as one of the great founders of literary modernism by critics who insisted that his politics had nothing to do with his art. Only very recently have critics begun to question this literary judgement. Findley shows many sides of the actual Pound in his fictional version — Pound's satiric insights, lyrical creations of beauty, sense of humour, racism, irrationalities, and violent hatreds — without attempting to reconcile or justify them.

Yet Pound's story frames Mauberley's in important ways. Many of the novel's epigraphs come from Pound's poem *Hugh Selwyn Mauberley*. This poem is generally read as Pound's satiric rejection of an earlier part of himself, personified as "Mauberley." It dramatizes what Pound perceived to be "a conflict between the antithetical demands of aestheticism and politics" (Ruthven 126) and, according to some, records Mauberley's tragedy as that of "the *pure* aesthete"

46

(Fraser 62). Its mode is ironic and, as Kuester suggests, functions as "a series of intertextual parodies in its own right" (87). Findley's use of epigraphs from this poem and others by Pound to frame his narrative in *Famous Last Words* raises the possibility of further ironies and parodic inscriptions. Critics disagree about how to read Findley's reinscription of the poem (in fragments as epigraphs to various chapters, in imagery, and in verbal echoes) and of the character of Mauberley himself. Whether the parody leads us to question Mauberley's integrity or to revise our understanding of what Mauberley might mean is a much debated topic. The signals in the text are mixed, but ultimately Findley appears to reclaim Mauberley as an embodiment of the possibility that Pound rejected too hastily. Scobie concludes a lengthy analysis with the following assessment: "So what distinguishes Findley's Mauberley, ultimately, from Pound's is the greater strength, thoroughness, and — it may be argued — heroism of his bearing witness" (209). Findley's Mauberley is more fully developed and allowed more scope for his defence. The work of art that gives him life is roomier, more complicated, and more fully fleshed out. His "bearing witness" is not confined to rules of courtroom relevance: it includes many apparently inconsequential details and incidents of sly humour that flesh out what in Pound is really a dismissive caricature.

Findley's evidently serious purpose in resurrecting Mauberley should not blind us to the very real sense of pleasure activated by the play with echoes of Pound's words. If Pound is also on trial, then the resonance of his imagery and the sharp insight into aspects of his age do much to redeem him in Findley's eyes. Findley "went through five whole modes" in writing *Famous Last Words* before he rediscovered the character of Mauberley in Pound's poem and realized that he was "the perfect voice to narrate the story" (*Inside Memory* 177). He is perfect for this role because his name reminds us that he is a borrowed fictional creation and not a real person. He is taken from art, not from life. His status as a fictional construct, as an imagining of alternative possibility, stresses Findley's belief in the power of the imagination to construct, and to alter, reality. Findley develops many of Pound's phrases in his creation of Mauberley's personality and story. He takes unflattering summations of Mauberley's life from Pound's poem, such as "Nothing, in brief, but maudlin confession, / Irresponse to human aggression" (75) and

"I was

"And I no more exist;

"Here drifted

"An hedonist." (77)

He then tests them against his fuller rewriting, which allows for these criticisms but which insists that they cannot tell the whole story.

In keeping with the theme of writing of trial, each Poundian epigraph invoked in *Famous Last Words* raises questions about the appropriate relation between art and reality. The first, *"The age demanded an image / Of its accelerated grimace . . ."* (3), asserts that the times favoured a mimetic role for art, a role in which art mirrors reality in all its speed and ugliness rather than providing an alternative image of eternal repose and beauty. In his commitment to the latter, Mauberley seems out of tune with his times. As Findley's Pound notes, "Mauberley's whole and only ambition is to describe the beautiful" (5). Yet that desire for order paradoxically leads him into the fascist camp, which eventually betrays the dream that he cherishes.

The second epigraph also stresses paradox: *"Elysium, though it were in the halls of hell . . ."* (37). The idea of a false heaven and haven, the lure of a false dream of perfection, obsesses Mauberley. He idealizes an unworthy woman, Wallis Simpson, and he abandons the integrity of Diana Allenby and Isabella Loverso to follow her fake glitter into disaster. The hotel Elysium, filled with ghosts and floating above the mountains, proves another mirage: its haven, a hell.

The third epigraph is similar in its juxtapositioning of the true artist, with his laurel wreath bestowed in ancient times by Apollo, the Greek god of the arts, against the *"tin wreath"* (59) awarded by popular acclaim in more decadent times to the less worthy recipient. Appropriately, Mauberley notes that Wallis's smile was "battered out of tin" in her early days in China (75). He notes the artificiality, but he responds to her signs of suffering and her clinging to life in spite of its treacheries. She is perhaps the artist most deserving of Pound's *"tin wreath,"* she who is not *"god, man or hero"* (59), only an ambitious woman seeking to make her way in a man's world.

The fourth epigraph, from Pound's contemporary W.H. Auden, an antifascist poet, articulates the nightmarish alienation of sequestered hatreds as the Second World War begins. Irony is replaced by clarity.

48

The *"accelerated grimace"* of the age yields to the clear-eyed recognition that *"Intellectual disgrace / Stares from every human face"* (157).

The epigraph to chapter 5 turns from the times to the artist, repeating one of Pound's more famous pronouncements: *"End fact. Try fiction"* (218). The lines between fact and fiction are blurred in Findley's text as Mauberley, the narrator, and the readers comb both in search of the truth. Yet *Famous Last Words* clearly attempts to put Pound's maxim into practice. The history that it records cannot be understood through a recounting of facts alone; like Pound, Findley puts his faith in a fictional re-creation that can make events come alive again and old debates seem relevant once more.

I have already discussed the biblical epigraph to chapter 6 in relation to the sky writing of de Broca. The epigraph to chapter 7 returns to Pound on the artist: *"The stylist has taken shelter, / Unpaid, uncelebrated . . ."* (293). Mauberley the stylist, alone in the deserted hotel, devotes himself to writing an increasingly damning story. Free of others' attentions, he can devote himself to recording his version of the truth. In the epigraph to chapter 8, the outside world intrudes once more to disrupt the artistic order that he has created. Metaphorically put, *"The Coral isle, the lion-coloured sand / Burst in upon the porcelain reverie . . ."* (323). This chapter records the murder of both Sir Harry Oakes in Nassau and Mauberley in Austria. The dream of perfection, *"the porcelain reverie,"* is shattered by the violences that it has unleashed. Mauberley's sense of himself as a bystander rather than an actor is also shattered in these scenes.

The epigraphs not only recall the works from which they have been taken but also frame possible readings of the new contexts in which they have been placed. Because Pound and his work are so much a part of Mauberley as Findley imagines him, the epigraphs also work to reinforce Mauberley's view of events. Mauberley tends to see things through the images conjured up by Pound's words, even when he finally rejects Pound's point of view. As he puts it, Pound "owns half my mind" (79).

Their affinity, and their dangerous blindness to the implications of their flirtations with fascism, are signalled by the horrific image of the one-eyed man, invoked metaphorically to account for Pound's apparent madness and then parodied in Mauberley's murder via an ice pick through his eye. Before narrating his break with Pound,

Mauberley justifies Pound's work as an unpleasant but necessary witness to the mad violence of the world, to "the world of chaos, fire and rage" unleashed during the Second World War. He suggests that Pound will be condemned because most people do not want to see what Pound sees: "the whispers of chaos, fire and anger in themselves" (77). Pound's broadcasts spoke to such urges and sought to inflame them, but his poetry works in more complex and often obscure ways. Therefore, it seems to me that Mauberley's apology for Pound is only partly convincing. He was not just the witness of doom; he sought to hasten its arrival and direct its energies against certain vulnerable groups in society in what can only be called a racist way.

Yet what we learn from Pound's tragedy is a lesson in humility rather than pride. His intolerance, his closing of his mind to other perspectives, is saddening and frightening. His story, as narrated by Findley, shows us how the imagination, the sole thing that keeps us alive and human, can be shut down, even in someone acknowledged to be a great artist. What does it mean when a great imagination is lost? Later, the systematic destruction of Hess's mind provides an eerie, horrific double of the symbolism of this scene. And both are echoed in Quinn's search to

> understand how Mauberley, whose greatest gift had been an emphatic belief in the value of the imagination, could have been so misguided as to join with people whose whole ambition was to render the race incapable of thinking. . . . (48)

For Findley, to close down the imagination is the greatest evil that one can direct against another human being. And Pound directs this evil against himself. He metaphorically blinds himself to what is happening around him, and he wilfully brainwashes himself to accept Nazi and Fascist propaganda as his only reality.

In a scene imagined by Findley, Mauberley and Pound end their long friendship. They argue about what is happening to their world. Findley parodies Pound's wordplay, admonitions, and adoption of dialect, and he invents an encounter with a cat to summarize, heavy-handedly, the perversity of Pound's behaviour. The cat stands in metonymically for his imagination; in captivity, Rudolf Hess becomes a cat in behaviour and self-identification as his humanity and sanity are methodically destroyed. Mauberley ends the scene with this moral: "That's right, I think. *First you feed it, then you kill it. Like your mind.* And mine. If I let you" (83). Hess lets them; Mauberley does not.

This scene poses one of the puzzles that the novel tries to piece together. Why would someone as talented as Pound choose to align himself with violence, propaganda, petty prejudices, and simplistic conspiracy theories? Why would he reduce the complexity of the world to a false choice between "the world of men at arms" and "the world of men in white linen suits" (82), especially when he was aware of many alternative possibilities? Mauberley rejects Pound's reading of the world and their times, but he is still unable to produce an alternative reading that goes beyond Pound's limiting terms.

The following scene shows Mauberley breaking with friends on the opposite side of the political spectrum, the antifascists Ned and Diana Allenby. The treatment of Ned shows the fallacy in Mauberley's earlier defence of Pound. Although Mauberley has suggested that Pound will be vilified for showing people what they do not want to see, Pound not only survived the war but also enjoyed the reputation of a great writer despite his diatribes against the Jews. On the other hand, Ned, who speaks up against the concentration camps when it is seen as impolite to acknowledge their existence (88), is murdered by the Nazis and forgotten by history. His is the true witnessing, the true act of bravery. He is also the better reader of history and of his friend Mauberley.

Ned suggests that Mauberley is attracted to fascism because, as "some kind of pilgrim looking for a faith," he has made the mistake of "looking for it under rocks" (88). His reading of Mauberley is confirmed when he and Diana leave. Only Mauberley's memory of Allenby's words prevents him from following the young Blackshirt whom he admires, yet he admits: "And I went away with him — in my mind. And knelt before his strength. And his victory" (91). Pound's distinction between men in uniforms and men in suits proves false here. Mauberley, like Pound, has been seduced by the Nazi myth of "the triumph of power" (Sontag 313). We will examine what Susan Sontag terms "fascist aesthetics" in the fourth section. Here it is sufficient to note how Findley makes use of competing readings of an action to encourage us to participate more actively in making sense of his text. In looking at the Blackshirts, Ned sees the lowest forms of life, metaphorically comparable to things that hide under rocks and fear the light; but Mauberley sees in the same men a compellingly primitive form of raw masculinity and an image of power. These competing interpretations of the Nazi myth form the substance of the history that Findley recreates in *Famous Last Words*.

Each scene of reading that the novel depicts enacts the process of puzzling out meaning individually, a process in which Findley hopes to engage us. The references to other works of art, the epigraphs, and the complex use of Pound's life and work suggest possible ways of entering and making sense of this difficult novel. At the same time, the cinematic methods of staging scenes of debate, dramatizing conflict through argument and imagery, and juxtaposing scenes that mirror and complicate one another replay history as if it were a film in which gestures and dialogue are more important than cause and effect. History becomes a kind of collage, multiplying its images more through cumulative, cross-referenced visual and aural images than through a linear development. The following section deals more closely with Mauberley's representation of history as myth, demonstrating how references to historical events are filtered through the grid of imposed mythological patterns and what that means for Mauberley's defence of the writer's craft.

"THE MYTHOLOGY OF NOW"

According to Findley, "Mauberley is endlessly fascinated with what he calls 'the mythology of now' . . ." (*Inside Memory* 191). His "mythology of now" refers to his sense that he and his coconspirators in the Penelope cabal are not only making history but also shaping public perceptions of what history means. He thinks of himself as living among larger-than-life personalities, people whose lives will be seen as mythic by both their contemporaries and future generations. That thinking is partly mistaken. His companions are ordinary people, not the gods he sometimes thinks them. But they do long for mythic status, and Mauberley tries to create it for them through his writing.

In creating *Famous Last Words*, Findley also engages in the creation and deconstruction of a "mythology of now." The mythology of his (and our) time demonizes or ridicules fascists, exploiting them as comic figures of fun or as erotic figures of desire. Think of the Nazis in the television show *Hogan's Heroes* or in movies such as Spielberg's *Indiana Jones and the Holy Grail* or Cavani's *The Night Porter*. These mythologies tend to deny Nazi humanity (and therefore their affinity with the rest of us) just as effectively as did their elevation to the status of supermen or gods in their own propaganda machines during the war. Findley's mythology therefore both embraces Mauberley's and throws it into question. It enacts a double engagement: with the mythology of the past (Mauberley's "now") and with that of the present, which is also double (the time of the book's publication — 1981 — and the time of its reading, a new "now" for each of us).

Mauberley casts the lives of the characters in his testament as contemporary versions of the classical Greek myths. But as Roland Barthes points out, myth is also "a mode of signification, a form" (109), which, he argues, "transforms history into nature" (129) and depoliticizes speech (143). Mauberley's mythologizing of history works as a naturalizing rhetoric that makes fascism seem both ordinary and thrillingly exotic. It downplays political motivations in favour of the psychological. The frame narration tends to mirror these tendencies in Mauberley's account rather than placing them in a larger social perspective. The effects of such narrative decisions will be examined more closely in the next section.

Every critic writing on *Famous Last Words* has discussed its status as a kind of historical fiction that tends to blur the distinctions between fact and fiction in order to convey its author's notion of truth. In explaining his search for the proper mode in which to tell the story in *Famous Last Words*, Findley says that he came to realize that

this wasn't just the story of men and women — but of men and women and the gods to whom they are obedient; of the fates that rule their lives and of the fact that history is created through the enactment of symbolic gestures — and told best through the evocation of icons. So what I must do is transpose this story, which is history, into another key — which is mythology. (*Inside Memory* 191)

This approach sounds quite similar to that of fascist artists such as Leni Riefenstahl. The musical metaphors of transposition and key reveal Findley's interest in the artistic shaping of the way in which events are perceived. He searches history for what it can tell us about the present and about human nature in general; his interest in the past for its own sake, unlike a historian's, is minimal. His interest in symbolic meaning thus takes precedence in his narrative over establishing the facts of exactly what happened or showing how history works as a complex pattern of causation and reaction. History becomes a source for mythology, for the symbolic representation of eternal truths. Yet despite its subordinate status, it remains a challenge to certain mythologies and the mythologizing habit of mind. What happened still matters, but Findley knows that our only access now to that reality is through words and their organization into a narrative.

The transposition of history into mythology gives *Famous Last Words* its epic character, but it is also responsible for the critical disagreements about the novel's ultimate effectiveness. Few professional historians would agree that "history is created through the enactment of symbolic gestures." History may be perceived, in part, through such gestures, but few historians write history in this mode. The events of history and their narration participate in a far more dynamic and complicated process than this mode suggests. Findley's statement privileges form over process, timelessness above timeliness, and the abstract over the specific. Symbolic gestures are the stuff of art, particularly of dance and theatre; they select, stylize, and freeze certain moments by raising them above the movements of history. The evocation of icons performs a similar function. Symbolic gestures, such as the king's abdication or de Broca's bombarding the Nassau garden party with antifascist brochures (the first an actual event, the second an imagined one), may take on larger significance in the eyes of those who make and record them, but their actual influence on the course of events is far from certain.

Similarly, an icon such as the king may symbolize power in some generalized way, but it is not a power with any real scope in the twentieth century. We can accept these symbols as embodying meaning within the narrative, but their relation to history is evocative rather than primary. They may seem to sum up an age and its priorities; they are less convincing when presented as either influential or all-encompassing in explanatory power.

Mauberley's account of the arrival of the *Nahlin* at Dubrovnik therefore seems unduly grandiose and even a little deluded in its attempt to mythologize the Windsors. With the benefit of hindsight, we now see them as minor figures. In their time, they did capture the imagination of many, but what they symbolized was the glamour of a public love affair, not the ability to make history. They renounced public duties for private satisfactions. Findley imagines what might have happened if that renunciation were only a façade for a secret grab at more power through the Nazis. If they had continued to seek political influence after the abdication through such dubious means, then their failure might be seen as tragic, he implies. *Famous Last Words* traces an imaginary trajectory for the couple from the golden promise of "this Dalmatian Camelot" (64) in Dubrovnik to its defeat on the ironically named ship *Excalibur*. Findley's problem, however, is that he can only reimagine actual personalities within the limits that they have established. To mythologize the Windsors, he needs to present them as significant people, and all the evidence suggests that they were not. The Windsors were celebrities, rich and famous, like movie stars. There is little in this narrative or in historical accounts of their lives to suggest that they were anything more. Yet Mauberley insists that "This was the new mythology. . . . Homer might have written it" (63). Mauberley is blinded by the glamour of celebrity, but Quinn, reading his narrative and knowing what it has led to, seems more interested in Mauberley the man than in the mythology that he has tried to create. These Homeric references say more about the ambitions of the Windsors and their admirers than they do about their potential or their achievement. These icons and their grand, symbolic gestures often fall flat. Findley reveals the scheming and the personal insecurities behind this supposedly Homeric love affair, demythologizing the mythology as Mauberley creates it.

In this sense, Mauberley's mythologizing of the Windsors back-fires. It casts them in an ironic rather than an aggrandizing mode. His inflation of their significance, through mythic comparison, high-lights their pettiness. The double reference of his description of Wallis Simpson in the lobby of the Imperial Hotel in China encodes his ambivalence about what myth she may be enacting. He writes of the "lacquered chair on which she sat" (70), an image that recalls not only Shakespeare's mythical Egyptian queen, Cleopatra, but also the complaining modern woman in T.S. Eliot's poem *The Waste Land*. Wallis is presented as veiled, with a face "like a mask" (68). In recording his lifelong infatuation with her, Mauberley writes that "It is only now — after twenty years — that I see her face as lacquered; only now that I realize she has never lived without the application of a mask." As the masked woman of Mauberley's thriller, she retains her mystery for him until the end. The image of the mask also highlights the theatricality of her world, a world of high stakes and large gestures, the world of myth. She is presented as "an expert: her mouth, her eyes, her hair were masterpieces of illusion . . ." (73). She has made herself the mythic "other woman" of adulterous desire.

For Findley, "A myth is not a lie, as such, but only the truth in larger shoes. Its gestures are wider. Its voice is projected to cover distance. . . . It is the ultimate theatre of human intrigue" (*Inside Memory* 191). Such a view of narrative has its attractions, but it also has its drawbacks. The "truth in larger shoes" may seem incongruous, absurd, or incomplete. (We may remember Little Nell's epiphany before his death, that "God's shoes were size twelve" [287], too big for Nelson Kelly, the little man who fails to sell his story of doom in time.) The same seems true for the Duke and Duchess of Windsor: each is too small a person for the iconic roles that they seek to play in the drama of history. They are too small for their mythic shoes. By casting their story in mythic terms, Findley reveals their humanity. Their failed attempts to make their lives fit mythic dimensions have tragic consequences for both themselves and those around them.

The mythological mode thus reveals the tragedy of false aspirations to superhuman status, showing how people always fall short of their ideals. But it also diminishes the role of human agency in history. By invoking gods and fate, Findley allows Mauberley and his fellow fascists off the hook of personal responsibility for the evils done in the name of fascism. Yet books are often more complex than their author's commentary on them. Although Mauberley and the frame narrator intermittently cast this story in the timeless mode of Greek myth, their mythologizing is balanced by the historical details that ground the narrative in the more specific modes of literary realism and individual personality. The book enacts a tension between the historical and the mythological; it does not completely transpose the one into the other.

Isabella Loverso is created with such loving accuracy that she survives Mauberley's attempt to aestheticize her out of reality into an allegorical representation of female sacrifice. When he responds to the tragedy and courage of her earlier life with the label "Andromache" (162), in reference to the tragedy of *The Trojan Women*, he may think that he is elevating her to a superhuman realm as a tribute, but he is denying her individuality, unique humanity, and suffering, denying as well his own partial responsibility for her final fate. He seems to be confirming the definition of her life that she has tried not only to acknowledge but also to fight, the idea that she can be seen as "The spoils of war" (162). Her phrase, and his choice to confirm it by responding with "Andromache," seals her fate in his mind as mythical allegory rather than as a woman who makes political choices and accepts full responsibility for her actions. But there is enough in the text about her political activism to enable us to see the inadequacies of the mythological label. She intervenes in the narrative and changes history by ensuring that the Windsors are delivered back to the British. She pays for this action with her life. She can be neither explained nor contained by Mauberley's label.

The same tension emerges in his account of Lord Wyndham's death. He highlights his ambivalence about the intimate yet distanced role that he plays as a voyeur, gently mocking his alternating attraction to, and repulsion from, the lives of the great: "I could hardly bear to watch. (But I always do.)" (92). The wicked humour at his own expense is typical. But as usual, he subordinates the individual who is dying before his eyes to the symbolic significance of the event. He transposes this man, Isabella's lover and Diana's father, into an icon of passing eras. Mauberley reacts not to the person or his dying but to the public significance that he sees in him. As the only deathbed scene set in a bed proper, this moment appropriately marks the end of an era. He writes: ". . . I realized I was kneeling more in awe of history than of death. . . . Somewhere a clock was striking. The reigns of Victoria, Edward, George rose up and fell away in seconds" (92–93). Here history is seen to live through individual memory and to die when the remembering witness to history dies. To Mauberley, Lord Wyndham is an icon of an era, but to Isabella he is the man who saved her from dying of grief when her husband and children were murdered, and to Diana he is a father. He may be an icon, but he is also much more.

In this scene, we learn the truth of what Quinn suggests, that myth can distort and deny history but also recall it. Lord Wyndham need not have existed for his fictional embodiment to symbolize the passing of an era. The fictional character can bring the historical record to life. Or, as Quinn tells Freyberg, "Mythology can have two meanings. . . . The Trojan War did happen" (150). Several levels of debate are engaged here. There is argument about what did and did not happen during the Second World War. The Holocaust has been extensively documented, yet some (as Freyberg predicts) continue to deny that historical reality. On that level, the distinctions between fact and fiction seem quite clear to most people; on other levels, however, the distinctions begin to blur. The sympathies of the Duke and Duchess of Windsor for the fascist cause are well known; whether or not they ever acted on those sympathies remains a matter of speculation. Some scenes in the novel recall matters of historical record; others seem plausible, but without a factual basis; still others are obviously inventions.

This technique encourages speculation about the areas of overlap between fiction and history, especially when both rely on techniques of narration, but it also encourages investigation of the genuine differences between the two. E.F. Shields argues that, "At the same time that Findley forces us to look at the facts of history, he uses his fiction to raise questions concerning the supposed factuality and objectivity of history itself" ("Mauberley's Lies" 48). From that point of view, Findley sees history as narrative and uses myth to expose the limitations of history as it is usually written. But he also holds myth up to the scrutiny of history, insisting that facts and truths exist beyond human manipulations of whether or not they get told. Shields concludes that, "while Findley uses his fiction to emphasize that the difference between fact and fiction is not always clear or even possible to determine, he does not reject the idea that there is a difference" (56). Indeed, that difference remains central to his project.

It was Findley's discovery of photographs of Dachau, before their general release to the public, in the living room of a Hollywood writer and producer, that led to his prolonged grappling with the problems given shape in *Famous Last Words*. As he puts it in *Inside Memory*,

How can this be explained to those who were not alive before that time: before there was a war, before there was a Dachau, before there was a Bomb? . . . Even in a world where Nagasaki and Hiroshima, Dachau and Auschwitz are names that tell of horrors distant as the Inquisition, it cannot be told what it meant to see those photographs that night. (31)

This is the impossible yet necessary task that Findley sets for himself in writing *Famous Last Words*: to tell what cannot yet must be told if the human race is to survive into the future. His telling was profoundly influenced by the circumstances of his discovery of what was at that time little known. The photographs had not yet been published. He points out: "I was looking into hell — and hell was real. And I saw all this in *Hollywood, California* . . ." (310). The contrast between the fabrication of dreams and images perfected in Hollywood and the construction of horror perfected in the Nazi death camps forces consideration of what links these two realities as well as of what separates them. *Famous Last Words* takes on this task. The Duke and Duchess of Windsor live Hollywood-style lives, yet they dine and party with fascists. The Spitfire Bazaar embodies this contradiction in dramatic form. What was designed as a public-relations coup, projecting the myth of the duchess as a potential queen, ends in nightmare as the underlying reality of her political affiliations is revealed.

Findley wants the perception of these links to take place within us at the personal level at which they first hit him, prompting self-discovery, and at a more distanced intellectual level, prompting a searching of the past for what has enabled such horror. In human terms, Findley concludes that this revelation of horror links him, through both revulsion and recognition, to the rest of the human race: "We are all a collective hiding place for monsters" (*Inside Memory* 311). If we cannot accept that possibility, then we will not find the compassion and strength to begin again. That self-searching requires historical searching. The past cannot be forgotten; it must be understood. Therefore, *Famous Last Words* seeks meaning in mythology and in history, exploring both systems of representation for the seeds of understanding, navigating, and surviving the mythological hell revealed in the photographs of the actual camp named Dachau.

Famous Last Words looks back on the events of the Second World War from the vantage point of approximately forty years later. Duffy argues that historical novels "teach readers that what they thought was temporally distant is morally contiguous, but that message begins in remoteness." For him, "the otherness of that past" is "more a matter of attitude than of a count of years" (*Sounding the Iceberg* iv). The horror of the death camps and the emergence of the Cold War combined to turn the historical realities of the Second World War into the material of mythology very quickly. The era seems remote in actuality, yet it is ever-present in films, television, plays, and books as something that we pretend to have put behind us morally but that fascinates us still.

Like most historical novels, *Famous Last Words* presents documented events beside invented ones and actual characters beside fictional ones. Traditionally, historical novels have included real figures in their narratives, but these figures have usually had walk-on parts in the lives of a central fictional character. That character plays a marginal role in the documented events of history, experiencing their impact and to some extent influencing their outcome without entering the official historical record. Findley remains true to that traditional pattern in his presentation of Mauberley, but he diverges from it when he invents complex emotional lives and private scenes of dialogue for his historical figures, many of whom were still alive when he wrote the novel. These inventions blur the boundary between history and fiction.

Hutcheon observes that "Past events are given *meaning*, not *existence*, by their representation in history." Recognizing this distinction, Findley focuses in *Famous Last Words* "in a very self-reflexive way on the processes of both the production and the reception of paradoxically fictive historical writing" (*Politics* 82). In the previous section, "Scenes of Reading," I focused on the complexities of reception generated by this kind of fiction, in which we are actively invoked to play a crucial interpretative role. In this section, I investigate the conditions of production. As Hutcheon points out,

> language constitutes reality, rather than merely reflecting it. . . .
> To write history — or historical fiction — is equally to narrate,
> to reconstruct by means of selection and interpretation. History
> (like realist fiction) is *made* by its writer, even if events are made

to seem to speak for themselves. Narrativization is a central form of human comprehension. ("Canadian Historiographic Meta-fiction" 231–32)

By focusing on the fabrications in *Famous Last Words* and its containment of Mauberley's story, Findley highlights their construction as narratives. Events are seldom allowed "to seem to speak for themselves." As we saw in the last section, epigraphs, intertextual references, and other framing devices draw attention to the work of reception, of making sense of any reported action. The novel also repeatedly draws attention to the work, especially the selectivity, initially involved in the production of narrative. Comically, but with a sting at the end of his tale, Mauberley records how omissions can shape a narrative to the teller's advantage:

> ... Wallis told the story of her life and left out China. I was very hurt. Then the Duke told the story of his life and left out having abdicated. Wallis was very pleased. Nonetheless these stories told the temper of the times and the motto we had adopted: *the truth is in our hands now.* (177)

Some biases may be deliberately introduced into a narrative, as in these examples; others may enter inadvertently, through ignorance or inaccurate assumptions about what to expect. Later, at a fascist dinner for the duke and duchess, Mauberley thinks that he is experiencing "history as she is never writ." He muses that some future historian will record his own imagined version of this dinner and will inevitably "get it wrong." The historian will see premeditation, calculation, and a plotted conspiracy where Mauberley sees only fortuitous chance. Historians, he thinks, "will not acknowledge that history is made in the electric moment, and its flowering is all in chance. . . . There is more in history of impulse than we dare to know" (180).

Although there is surely some genuine insight in this observation, there is also the self-justification that tinges all Mauberley's writing. If history is all impulse and chance, then his own responsibility for what has happened is greatly diminished. Such a vision downplays his responsibility in calling for the kind of strong leadership that Hitler and Mussolini offered. But in excusing him, this vision of history also makes the possibility of any human action for change seem deluded or ineffective. *Famous Last Words* is dedicated to showing that words and deeds can make a difference, and therefore Mauberley's insight here is qualified because there *is* a purpose behind the dinner, a purpose that may have taken shape through a lucky combination of accident and desire but that results in the formation of the Penelope cabal.

The Penelope Cabal

In "Mauberley's Lies," Shields documents the various sources on which a case for the existence of such a plot might be built, stressing the possible motives of the writers of various German documents about the Windsors, the Windsors' own accounts, and those of various historians; the intended audiences of these different versions; and the crucial role of interpretation in assigning them significance. Although the Penelope cabal is Findley's invention, it arises logically enough from some accounts of the Windsors' close relations with various Nazis. The cabal's chief significance, however, is mythic rather than historical. Duffy sees it as "no more than a plotting device, a way of involving Mauberley within a broad context of events and personalities and of finally getting him off stage" ("Let Us Compare Histories" 199). But its function cannot be limited to plot alone. It carries intertextual references that expand the range of Mauberley's story, complicating and enriching its meaning.

As Kuester points out, Pound's *Hugh Selwyn Mauberley* is "based on the *Odyssey* in a way similar to Joyce's 'parodic' use of Homer" (87–88). In Pound's poem, Mauberley's "true Penelope was Flaubert" (Pound 61; see also 71); that is, Mauberley's one true love is his art, the art of choosing exactly the right word for the idea or the emotion that he wishes to convey. Findley's use of Pound's Odyssean motifs suggests that Mauberley betrays his vocation as an artist and his dedication to beauty, his "true Penelope," for the false Penelope of political involvement in the shady machinations of the cabal.

Reading literally, Kuester sees Mauberley as "hardly an Odysseus character: born in a Boston hotel, he does not have an ancestral home to return to, and his Penelope leads him into death" (88). But there are parallels linking Mauberley to Odysseus. Like Joyce's Ulyssean Bloom, Mauberley is a permanent exile, wandering the world, and like Joyce's Ulyssean Stephen, he seeks a father rather than a wife. His story parodies the classical myth in the modernist mode. For Mauberley, home is no longer, like Odysseus's Ithaca, a place awaiting his return; symbolized by "Penelope," it has become an ideal, to be realized through art or politics and, ultimately, through an aestheticized politics — fascism. Wallis agrees to see herself as Penelope because the myth seems to justify her wish to be queen at any cost. She sees her husband as an Odyssean figure because she feels that he has been forced to abdicate, abandoning his throne and country to marry her in exile when, from her point of view, he should have been allowed to make her queen. The goal of the plot is to restore both of them to the throne of England, their Ithaca. But unlike Odysseus, they would exercise only a puppet's power, remaining indebted to the Nazis who would have reinstalled them there. The logic of the myth would cast Mauberley among the false suitors to Penelope's hand in the absence of her husband. But this logic is twisted by the historical realities. These human characters cannot live up to their mythic roles. The duke is a pathetically weak creature, no match for the wily Odysseus: a pawn rather than an agent in his restoration. His wife assumes the Odyssean role of regaining power through intrigue and guile.

As in much modernist writing, the mythic references expose the degraded nature of modern life. There are no more heroes. Findley suggests that this failure resides in a confusion of fact and fiction, of the human and the mythic, rather than in inherent differences between people now and then. Even when he was king, the duke was unable to accept the difference between his iconic and his human status. He confused his iconic status as Prince of Wales and then as king with his power as a human being.

The private interview between him and his mother, Queen Mary, pivots around their different understandings of the iconic power of the monarchy. Mauberley cannot have been present at this scene. He must have imagined it. It parallels his own final interview with his father. Once more a parent and child look down on the world from a great height before reaching a decision that will part them forever. Queen Mary shows her son a dressmaker's dummy of the queen. When he asks, "Is it you?", she replies, "It is the Queen" (103). Her answer distinguishes between who she is in herself and who she is in her symbolic role as royalty.

Through this symbol of the dummy, "her other self as if it were her twin," her "sawdust sister" (103), she dramatizes the limits of royal power to tell her son that he may keep Wallis as a mistress but that he cannot marry her. The icon has a role of its own, separate from human desires or needs. That mythic power, independent of human individuality or agency, is symbolized by its "leather facelessness" and its lack of arms and legs (103). As king, he cannot make a twice-divorced American woman his queen. The iconography will not allow it.

Given the choice of compromising and keeping her as his mistress or abdicating his kingship in order to marry her, he chooses, like Mauberley's father before him, the most extreme (and self-defeating) response available: to abdicate. Whereas Odysseus moves in and out of many disguises, the Duke of Windsor cannot accept that his power as king is not absolute but dependent on upholding the mythic status of a role untouched by scandal. But the duchess and the other plotters do understand this contingency. As Mauberley says, "It was the Crown she had married — we all knew that — only to have it whisked away." Ironically, her husband's abdication has deprived her of what she most wanted. When Mauberley remarks that she is "just like Penelope," still waiting for "the one true love of [her] life to return," he indicates that this love is the crown, not the duke (182). The Penelope cabal rewrites the Odyssean myth in these terms: in its version, Penelope and her suitors await the crown, not a returning Odysseus.

The duke's pathetic attempt to recreate the dressmaker's dummy of the queen as a gift for his wife in Nassau underlines the travesty that he and Wallis would have made of the crown. He sees that his creation is "a failure. Head and body could not be made one" (353). For all her skills as an actress, the duchess lacks the understanding of majesty that Queen Mary tries to show her son when she reveals her sawdust dummy in the tower. Elsa Maxwell, the superficial gossip columnist, is fooled by the dummy. Her comments underline the role that journalists play in advancing the mythology of royalty: "And oh — you should talk about 'majesty.' The way she stood there. The carriage. The bearing. The dignity. The dress. The hat . . ." (352). This is a comic scene, ironically repeating the duke's first encounter with the dummy. Elsa's conflation of "dignity" and "dress" shows how easily the trappings of power may be confused with the reality.

But the duke knows that he and his wife are fakes. When he burns the dummy the following day, the Penelope conspiracy is effectively killed. Although he had not been told of the cabal, his participation, when the time comes, is essential to its success. But in rejecting the dummy that he has tried to bring to life, he abdicates a second time. This time he renounces his dreams of a recovery. He has even lost his fragile belief in his God-given right to iconic status and in Wallis's natural suitability for it. In this scene, he finally recognizes that he cannot make his wife queen and that

> he was condemned forever to be hidden by the shadow of his wife: a shadow that would lengthen till it all but shuttered out his own: just as his mother's had . . . when she made him feed the birds and had left him there alone to find his way from a room without the benefit of lights. (354)

The duke comes to this understanding after the kidnapping attempt fails. To the Penelope cabal, he has always been a shadow, an iconic cipher to be manipulated as a cover for their own grab at power. His emptiness symbolizes the hollowness at the core of their venture, a flaw that they choose to ignore. He is the kingpin of their enterprise, yet he is not privy to their plans. In their terms, he is not "one of us," a phrase that echoes through all their plottings.

This cabal of conspirators, like most, sees the world in absolute terms, as a battle between "us" and "them." The admirable characters in the novel refuse these terms and the cabal that embodies them. The interview between Lindbergh and Allenby, another scene that Mauberley could not have witnessed directly, dramatizes a debate that has continued through Cold War and post-Cold War thinking. Lindbergh thinks simplistically: if Allenby is not with the Nazis and the Penelope cabal, then he must be "Some sort of Communist" (111). When Allenby claims the centre as his political space, Lindbergh insists that "There *is no centre*. There's nothing now but two halves: right and left. . . . Them and us. Nothing in between" (111–12).

This exchange enacts the central debate of the book, repeating the arguments between Quinn and Freyberg, Mauberley and Pound, in yet another forum. Allenby wishes to reject both of Lindbergh's halves, what he rephrases as "*barbarism* and *complete élitism*" (112), but he does not have the patience or the imagination to take this threat seriously enough. His wife sees that "Ugliness of spirit in other people bewildered him" (117). That bewilderment costs him his life.

Findley writes to persuade those of us like Allenby to go beyond our bewilderment with evil and to try to understand it more fully, because only through understanding can it be challenged and defeated. Ironically, the novel dramatizes how the two oppositions of Lindbergh's worldview are collapsed into one through their shared opposition to the compromises and subtleties of Allenby's position. Findley takes a fact from history — Lindbergh's quest "to invent a mechanical heart" (118) — and turns it into a metaphor for the inhumanity of the position that he represents in the novel (a position based on the political sympathies of the actual human being on which this fictional "Lindbergh" is modelled). He also shows that the result of the conspiracy's us-versus-them mentality is a narrowing of the circle of "us," for paranoia feeds on itself. First Allenby, identified as a potential supporter, must be killed when he rejects Lindbergh's invitation to join this anonymous but select group. Later, Isabella, Hess, and Mauberley himself are also destroyed by their own cabal.

It is at Allenby's funeral that Mauberley first sees Harry Reinhardt, though he does not yet know his name. Reinhardt becomes the embodiment of the dark side of the Penelope cabal and a living symbol of its conflation of barbarism and élitism. At one time, Findley thought of naming the book *"Alligator Shoes"* ("Long Live the Dead" 79; York, *Front Lines* 84), an apt image for the "compelling menace" embodied in this character (120) (and an appropriate, reversed image, perhaps, of God's size-twelve shoes). Mauberley describes Reinhardt's shoes as "Shiny shoes; glossy shoes; sensual shoes, if such a thing exists — but appropriate, I suppose, for walking in the mud. Alligator shoes" (121). Although the mud is real on the day of the funeral, the reference resonates with moral implications as well. Just as Mauberley seeks his ideal under rocks, so Reinhardt is at home in the mud. He becomes the nemesis, first for those, like Allenby, who refuse to join the Penelope cabal and eventually for those members who become disillusioned and seek to leave it, including Hess and, finally, Mauberley himself.

Ironically, the circle of "us" becomes smaller and smaller as suspicions grow. The mythical name Penelope proves appropriate, for each of the duchess's political suitors is killed to preserve her for her husband; ironically, whereas these killings ensure Odysseus's rein-statement in the original myth, they ensure the failure of the duke and duchess in their modern reenactment. The Penelope cabal begins in abdication and ends in betrayals: a fitting symbol of the worst excesses of what Pound's Mauberley calls "a botched civilization" (64).

Historical Puzzles: The Kidnapping Plot, Rudolf Hess, and Sir Harry Oakes

As Shields explains, in reading *Famous Last Words* "we are surprised again and again by the unexpected factuality of many of the charac-ters and events as well as by the accuracy of many of the details" ("Mauberley's Lies" 46). Many of what seem to be fantastic details in Findley's recounting of the German plot to kidnap the Duke and Duchess of Windsor in Portugal, the bizarre and unsolved murder of Sir Harry Oakes, and the puzzling story of Rudolf Hess's flight to England on 10 May 1941 have been borrowed from historical accounts. Many of the details in Peter Allen's *The Crown and the Swastika: Hitler, Hess and the Duke of Windsor*, though it was published after Findley's novel (in 1983), correspond with what is reported in it. Findley's innovation is in imagining solutions to these mysteries, which historians have been unable to resolve through the sifting of contradictory and inadequate evidence. Findley assigns meaning to each of these mysterious events by threading them together into his fictional story of the Penelope cabal. Each of these "historical puzzles" (Shields, "Mauberley's Lies" 49) is made expli-cable through its place in the expanding web of the Penelope con-spiracy. In real life, conspiracy theories often seem absurdly paranoid, simplistic explanations of complex events, but in fiction, we allow more leeway for such a heavy reliance on plot and plotting.

THE KIDNAPPING PLOT

In Findley's version, the kidnapping plot involves an internal Ger-man rivalry between two top Nazi figures and their organizations: Schellenberg, head of the Reich Central Security Office on the Albrechtstrasse, whom Findley puts outside the cabal, and von

Ribbentrop, head of the Foreign Office on the Wilhelmstrasse, who is part of it. In the end, Schellenberg defeats von Ribbentrop, and the Penelope conspiracy is over, but as Findley tells it, neither wins in the manoeuvrings around the kidnapping plot. Isabella Loverso is responsible for betraying the cabal and warning the British authorities in time to prevent the kidnapping. She pays for this act with her life, killed by von Ribbentrop. As each member of the cabal falls under suspicion of betrayal, the supposedly clear divisions between "them" and "us" are blurred.

In each of these stories of betrayal, Findley focuses on the waste and destruction wreaked by misplaced ambitions and misused creative talents. Many innocent people, including children, are killed to satisfy the egotistical drives of the Nazis, their collaborators, and the duchess. Despite receiving a warning to beware of British friends, she cannot know whom to trust in this context of intrigue. She thwarts Schellenberg's plans for the kidnapping, but at the cost of sabotaging von Ribbentrop's plan to use the kidnapping to keep the Windsors in Europe. Her action therefore leads to her banishment to the Bahamas.

Both Schellenberg and von Ribbentrop are described as artist figures: Schellenberg as "a master of deceit," becoming the characters that he plays, "much as an actor trained by Stanislavsky might do" (222), and von Ribbentrop as "a craftsman" in the field of diplomacy (235). Like them, the duchess thrives on creating and mastering illusion. But while she aspires to be a great actress, thinking of royalty as the ultimate role, the duke feels suffocated by the role that he must play. Free for a moment during the confusion on the night of the thwarted kidnapping, "he knew that for months he had worn his face like a garment. A woollen mask in which he had begun to suffocate" (212). Whereas the others misuse their talents to create illusions, the duke exchanges his suffocating mask of royalty for the mask of bandages that more truly reflects his state as a wounded, outcast king (237). Appropriately, his physical wounds, like his psychological ones, have been self-inflicted.

Findley invents the story of the duke's encounter with his mirrored selves as a fictional embodiment of the novel's obsession with the distortions of mimetic realism and as an oblique commentary on the multiple constructions of individual identity. This encounter is told indirectly, through the filter of the duke's nightmare on board the

American ship *Excalibur* on the way to the Bahamas. In a lengthy discussion of mirror imagery in the novel, Scobie points out that mirrors afford "images of a mediated vision of the self" (219). He argues that, in this complex encounter with his past and potential selves, the duke is responding to "fantasy selves" (222), to what I would term his iconic function in the past as the golden Prince of Wales and to his potential iconic status in the future as a symbol of glittering "splendour" (*Famous Last Words* 251). As Scobie notes, the duke himself assassinates this possibility of a future mythic status by running into this particular mirror. To underline the symbolic significance of this doubled gesture of abdication, Findley follows the destruction of the mirror with the sentence "*Excalibur* heaved" (252). As the ship heaves on the waves of the sea, the symbolic sword responds to the abdication of a British king.

Excalibur, the sword that legitimated King Arthur's rule and guaranteed his mythic status, proves an ironic name for the ship designated to take the Windsors to the Bahamas. This *Excalibur* takes this ex-king away from power and out of mythology. Unlike Arthur, the duke is an all-too-human figure. Drunkenly rebellious and wearing mascara in Portugal (191, 207), and heavily bandaged on board ship, he proves himself an inappropriate heir to the Arthurian tradition. His self-inflicted injury in the Martello tower of mirrors provides a fittingly absurd conclusion to a farcical evening, yet it has serious consequences for his own future and for those of the people caught up in the conspiracy.

The farce of the aborted dinner party is placed in perspective by the torture and murder of Maria da Gama, the little Portuguese girl who delivers the flowers with the warning note for Schellenberg (disguised as his alter ego Schaemmel). The Penelope plotters and their Nazi rivals leave destruction in their wake: the duke and duchess through an often criminal carelessness, Estrade and Schellenberg/Schaemmel with deadly intent. Their stories recall Isabella's earlier questions to Mauberley: "Are you afraid, my friend? Are you never afraid of what we do? Of the meaning of what we do and who we are?" (167). These are the questions that Findley hopes to prompt in us through the shocking juxtaposition of the farcical dinner party and its gruesome aftermath.

Quinn's dream after he has read this part of Mauberley's account makes Findley's purpose clear. His dream of clasping a dead Maria expands into a nightmare in which he lies "on a bed of corpses whose arms were wound around his back to hold him fast." The deadly story holds him in a similar grip. In the following line, his dream merges with the duke's: "And on the wall the dreamer lay bandaged and terrified, huddled under his blankets: lost at sea" (254). Both sympathy and condemnation are mixed in the pathos of this image. The duke has no moral bearings; he has lost authority and a personal sense of direction. This loss makes him dangerous to himself and others, but it also makes him an object of compassion. All of Findley's work burns to lead the lost back home. This is one of the most powerful images in his fictive vocabulary.

Here it links Quinn's sympathy for the lonely dog howling for a response, his fancy that Mauberley's words "must have poured from his brain" in "the way that howl was coming now from the dog down the mountain" (253), and his sympathy for the duke as yet another lost soul. His empathy for dog, writer, and banished king is balanced, however, by his admiration for the craft that has created this symbolic story from the bare facts of the failed kidnapping. Quinn's comparison of Mauberley's dream imagery with Shakespeare's (254) ensures that we remember that Mauberley has constructed any empathy that we feel, reminding us of his myth-making agenda and of Findley's own double agenda in placing Mauberley's "mythology of now" within the context of his own ironic and morally committed retelling. In terms of the epigraph from Thornton Wilder that precedes the novel proper, the story of the failed kidnapping challenges us to "lay down a stake" (n. pag.). It is impossible to remain indifferent to the immorality of the Penelope cabal. Each new incident of its evil pushes us further toward a revulsion that actively rejects such abuse of power, yet we retain sympathy for its increasing cast of human victims.

RUDOLF HESS

Although the duchess thinks her husband a fool, she herself is responsible for inadvertently betraying the cabal and thus prompting Hess's disastrous flight to Britain. The sheet of paper that Estrade steals from her, with "PENELOPE" and a crude drawing of von Ribbentrop's personal insignia on it (231), sets Hess's story in motion and eventually gives Schellenberg an advantage over von Ribbentrop. Her carelessness, greed, and indifference to the fate of others seem almost as culpable as the tortures that Schellenberg/Schaemmel and Reinhardt perpetrate. They certainly provide them with the excuse for further violence.

Findley's use of the duchess and the Penelope plot provides a fictitious reason for Hess's flight. But Findley's story begins with two paragraphs repeating the known facts before shifting into an obviously fictionalized account of the interview between von Ribbentrop and Hitler in reaction to the news.

Von Ribbentrop's "panic" in the interview (302) mirrors the duke's in the earlier mirror scene. Each man confronts unpleasant truths about the consequences of his earlier decisions in the "mirror" before him: the duke sees in his mirrors the result of his decision to abandon his iconic role as mythic figure, and von Ribbentrop sees in Hitler's face the enormity of what he has done in supporting a madman's rise to power. Both scenes recall Mauberley's moment of truth as he recognizes his face in the mirror in the crowded train of fleeing refugees after mistaking it for someone else's.

Hitler's madness finds its own refracted mirroring in the way that Hess's pretence of madness leads, under the direction of Reinhardt (posing as "the Keeper," Hart [308]), to the calculated destruction of his mind and the creation of a new identity for him as madman/cat. British and Nazis collaborate in this cover-up as they do earlier in the creation of the Penelope cabal. Findley takes certain details from the historical record—for instance, that Hess was a vegetarian before his flight to Britain but ate meat in prison there (Shields, "Mauberley's Lies" 49) — and transforms them into a horrifying indictment of military psychiatric practices. As is usual in his fiction, he implies that the true madmen are those who drive Hess mad. A world that condones and rewards such torture is a world itself gone mad — and fallen from grace. This is a theme developed more fully in *Head-hunter*.

Ironically, these barbarous practices are directed from the Eden Hotel, just as the Hotel Elysium seems to call attention to the irony of naming its particular hell a paradise. In these instances, Findley calls attention not only to humanity's fallen state, in Christian terms, but also to the treacheries of language, which deceives as readily as it reveals. Mauberley employs a similar technique in recording

71

Oakes's threat to the Windsors' plotted escape as a clever pun: "*Trips is an interesting word. . . . Thing is, some trips are journeys — and other trips are falls*" (365). As Mauberley's narrative demonstrates, the Windsors' abortive trip away from Nassau proves a final fall in its overreaching attempt to be an epic journey. The same language can be applied to Mauberley's life story: it also proves to be both journey and fall. A "fastidious dresser" all his life, Mauberley is reduced to wearing cast-off rags when he parts for the last time from his friends, the Pounds, who think that this once elegant figure now looks like "Dorothy's Scarecrow" (4). Dorothy is the name of Pound's wife, who gives Mauberley a bootlace to replace his missing tie, but her name is used here to invoke the epic journey in the Hollywood movie *The Wizard of Oz* as another context for understanding Mauberley's final journey as a quest for self-acceptance and, metaphorically, home. In these ways, even simple words carry multiple resonances that can create imaginative links between the unfamiliar and the known.

SIR HARRY OAKES

Once again, many of the details of Oakes's life and death, including some of the most unusual (such as his destruction of the trees that he had planted and the circumstances of his murder), are based on known facts: what Findley invents are a reason for the murder and a murderer, as well as scenes to flesh out these details. Just as he uses a howling dog to symbolize the Duke of Windsor's sense of abandonment and a ravenous cat to mark Hess's complete disintegration, so he has Mauberley summarize the meaning of Oakes's murder (and the book as a whole) in his anecdote of the person who has fallen or been pushed from the deck of a ferry and "eaten by a shark in full view of fifty or sixty people who all stood by and did nothing" (324). Mauberley himself, of course, stands by and does nothing for much of the narrative, until he feels himself pushed into taking a more active role in arranging the murder of Oakes. In throwing him to the sharks of the cabal, Mauberley knows that he himself must soon follow. His own leap is into complete submission to the sadistic Nazi Reinhardt (a human embodiment of the shark), whose power he has always worshipped.

Findley makes the mysterious murder of Oakes the climax of Mauberley's self-damning story and the final catastrophe in the defeat of the Penelope cabal. As the war progresses, the cabal fears that it is losing its chance to seize the initiative. In a reversal of Allied imagery, Mauberley characterizes the cabal's anxiety as a fear that "All the gains and benefits of years of Fascist control would be crushed beneath the heel of democracy" (337) if it does not act to preempt an Allied defeat of Mussolini with its own royal coup. That phrase, "the heel of democracy," renews the cliché of the crushing heel of dictatorship by reversing its attachment, destabilizing any comfort that we may have been feeling with Mauberley's narrative, and by its ironic redeployment reminding us of the larger political context in which this melodramatic story unfolds.

Mauberley weaves the story of Oakes into his personal mythology: Oakes reminds him of both his father and Pound, his surrogate father (356). In betraying his latest substitute father, he imagines himself following his father's advice and example. In killing the father at last, he frees himself to become the father. When he tells Reinhardt that he needs "a death," he concludes that "It was done. My fall was over. All the way down" (375).

More trivially, he imagines the Penelope plot as a boy's romantic adventure story and casts himself as the hero:

> Now, I thought, lifting the lid, I am playing d'Artagnan. And the Queen of France depends on my finesse.
> Oakes, when he entered, was hardly my image of the evil Lady de Winter, but he would do as one whose machinations could destroy a Royal House. (368–69)

This *Three Musketeers* style of rhetoric, with its absurd cross-gender casting of the rough-as-bags Oakes as the aristocratic Lady de Winter, punctures the self-importance of the cabal, rendering Mauberley more pitiful than evil. The derivative, recycled lie that he tries to run past Oakes (*"Illness — operation — Boston . . ."* [371]) shows how thoroughly corrupt and dead his imagination has become through his association with the fascist cause. When he attains his final humiliation, licking Reinhardt's hands clean of Oakes's blood (378), and then learning that all his efforts have been in vain because Schellenberg has thwarted their plans in Germany, his own story is almost over.

Mauberley's "mythology of now" begins with high ambitions and ends in defeat. The excitement of the *Nablin*'s triumphant entry into Dubrovnik finds its shadowy parallel and alter ego in the ship that awaits the Windsors' abortive flight from Nassau. Mauberley describes this last ship as "a sort of spirit-ship — a mirror ship, a spectre" (356). Its disappearance marks the end of mythologies of grandeur and the beginning of real life, with its own mythology of the mundane. As he imagines the duke and duchess abandoned in their rowboat on the empty sea, he shows the duchess realizing at last that "Whatever they were — here and now — the two of them — was exactly what they would be forever" (383). After conjuring up a possible history from the hints of historical evidence left as unfinished threads by professional historians, Findley returns his characters to the actual mythologies spun out of their reduced hopes by the resourceful Windsors: of everyday pleasures (cards, dead-heading roses, walking dogs) cast in the superior glow of knowing "what it was to have given everything away for love" (384). In the context that he creates for the duke's final sentiment, this myth of having sacrificed all for love can only be read ironically as face-saving self-deception.

A tougher problem for us is how to read Findley's own mythologizing of history in *Famous Last Words*. In this section, I have concentrated on how Findley interweaves fact and fiction to push us toward a sympathetic identification with the dilemmas of his characters and toward taking a stand on the moral issues that their lives and deaths raise. I have been concerned more with describing how the narrative is constructed than with assessing its style and how it works. With this groundwork established, the next section will evaluate some of Findley's more controversial stylistic innovations, symbols, characterizations, and plotting decisions.

FINDLEY'S INTERTEXTUAL STYLE

In previous sections, I have considered how *Famous Last Words* deploys its enabling metaphor of writing on trial to set its narrative in motion, stage scenes of interpretation and disputation, and extend the metaphor to put not only literature but also European civilization, politics, art, and history on trial. Now it is time to put the novel

74

itself on trial. I have discussed characterization, plotting, language, intertextual references, and imagery, but I have not given extensive consideration to how these elements are integrated into the novel's distinctive style. Critics agree in describing the stylistic mannerisms of *Famous Last Words*; where they disagree is in assessing their function. Hutcheon, Pennee, and York find a moral message in Findley's style; Williams finds a style offered in place of a morality (260). I see evidence for both positions in the text. We can conclude from this evidence either that the novel is morally confused or that the issues are too complex for final judgement. These debates may be clarified, if not resolved, by paying further attention to the novel's reinscriptions of fascist and postmodernist aesthetics, its exclusive reliance on psychological explanations for human relationships, and its dialogue with Canadian literary traditions.

"Fascist Aesthetics"

My reading of *Famous Last Words* has stressed its reliance on inter-textuality, by which I mean the way that one text assimilates, echoes, and incorporates words, images, and ideas from other texts. This is a simplified and utilitarian view of a term whose many disparate definitions play an important role in contemporary theory. Gener-ally speaking, intertextuality has replaced what used to be called source-influence studies with a way of thinking about relations among texts that, in Owen Miller's terms, "draws heavily on two basic principles: (1) a mosaic concept of the text as a series of quotations; (2) the inferential feature of presuppositions" (24). The focus of intertextual study thus falls on a text's relations to other texts (not just literary but also historical, cultural, and social ones) and on our perception of these relations. Knowledge of authorial intention becomes less relevant in this kind of reading than perception of intertextual echoes and how they function in their new context.

In the third section, I concentrated on literary intertextualities, and, in the fourth, on the interplay of mythological and historical ones. Throughout this study, I have referred to fascism as an important ideological intertext in *Famous Last Words*, but I wish to concentrate more fully here on what Sontag terms "fascist aesthetics" in her important article "Fascinating Fascism." In a review of *The Wars*,

Hulcoop draws attention to a potential in Findley's style for reinscribing a "fascist aesthetics" (119). His insight throws light on some disturbing scenes in the later novel.

Sontag asks two questions of particular relevance to *Famous Last Words*: "Why has Nazi Germany, which was a sexually repressive society, become erotic? How could a regime which persecuted homosexuals become a gay turn-on?" (323). *Famous Last Words* forces us to confront these questions through its portrayal of Mauberley's complicity with fascism and his masochistic fascination with the vicious Reinhardt. We may argue about whether the novel becomes complicit with the thinking that it questions or whether it always manages to maintain an ironic distance from Mauberley's involvement.

Dellamora argues that *Famous Last Words* is "complicit in an erotics of apocalypse that is both homophobic and homosexual. Mauberley's fantasy of fellating a Blackshirt . . . is only one such moment of ethical/political failure." It is unclear to me whether this failure is seen as exclusively Mauberley's or Findley's, or as something shared by both. To Dellamora, ". . . Findley faces the allegation (and the temptation) that to be homosexual is to lose one's humanity," but in facing them, and in inscribing them within the ironic "double talking, doubled discourses" of the novel (181), he moves beyond them to create a new space in which Mauberley can simultaneously speak both his homosexuality and his humanity. Dellamora acknowledges the risks that Findley takes, but he sees the novel as ultimately justifying them.

Let us examine these risks more closely. After suffering from writer's block through most of the story, Mauberley finds his voice after his assignation with Reinhardt, when he licks Oakes's blood from the murderer's hands. He then loses his life to the same avenging figure after his story has been told. The conjunction of violence, eroticism, creativity, and death is disturbing here. Can they be justified by Mauberley's honesty in confessing to such complicated, dark emotions and by his implicitly renouncing them as he gives shape to his story on the walls of Isabella's old room? Why does Mauberley smile as he thinks about sitting "amongst the *other* whores" (359) while he waits for his assignation with the messenger? Why should it please him to consider himself a prostitute and to revel in his survival when so many better people are dead? What inferences should we draw from his open admiration for Reinhardt's "damned beauty" (360) and from his associating it explicitly with maleness, darkness, and danger? And what about the role of the frame narrator in reinforcing these associations by assigning Reinhardt a mythic exit worthy of a dark romantic or fascist hero — "And the air was filled with crystal noise and a blowing avalanche into which Harry Reinhardt disappeared" (388–89) — after his brutal and prolonged murder of Mauberley and his papers?

Perhaps there are no clear answers to such questions. They point to contradictions that we can see but not easily resolve. The value of the book lies in the debates that it raises. Each of us must decide where the balance falls and whether contextual ironies sufficiently outbalance such apparently romantic endorsements of an erotics of violence. Sontag notes that "The solemn eroticizing of fascism must be distinguished from a sophisticated playing with cultural horror, where there is an element of the put-on" (322). Findley's learned play with various intertextualities, including the camp signs of fascist aesthetics, his wordplay, and his general self-consciousness seem to place his work in the category of sophisticated play. There is certainly an elaborate element of "put-on" in both the frame narrator's and Mauberley's style that inoculates us from the fascination that Mauberley feels for a character such as Reinhardt. Yet the intermittent reminders of the horrors of the death camps make such sophisticated play with horror seem obscene. How do we reconcile the put-on with that reality?

Sontag perceptively notes that, increasingly, contemporary people are encouraged "to regard their very lives as a (life) style." In such a world, sex becomes "a self-conscious form of theater, which is what sadomasochism is about: a form of gratification that is both violent and indirect, very mental" (325). This insight illuminates not only Mauberley's attraction to the Fascist Blackshirt and then to Reinhardt but also the theatrical lovemaking of the Duke and Duchess of Windsor before the framed photograph of Queen Mary on the *Excalibur* and in front of the dressmaker's dummy of the queen in Nassau. They cannot make love — if that is the right word in this context — without the queen as audience. Mauberley describes their lovemaking as a sadomasochistic ritual in which the duke humiliates himself in symbolically shaming his mother and revenging himself on both her and his wife simultaneously. Whereas the text seems ambivalent about Mauberley's erotic attractions, these scenes are more clearly negative, showing a sad and diminished sexuality. Both duke and duchess are wounded in this relationship. Is this only Mauberley's (outsider's) view of heterosexual lovemaking, or is it a more sweeping commentary on how the self-conscious theatre of the duchess and her circle corrupts everything that they touch? Again, we must decide, but the scales seem weighted toward the latter interpretation.

Although Mauberley's eroticizing of the Nazi menace is the clearest expression of fascist aesthetics in *Famous Last Words*, Findley seems to invoke other aspects of the genre in the staging of his novel. Sontag demonstrates exhaustively how "history become[s] theater" in Leni Riefenstahl's films (311). (Riefenstahl was the leading filmmaker in Nazi Germany, making films commissioned by the Nazis.) Mauberley and the Duchess of Windsor seek a similar transformation. Riefenstahl's defence of her work is identical to Mauberley's. She claims: "I am fascinated by what is beautiful, strong, healthy, what is living" (qtd. in Sontag 312). According to Sontag, "what she cares about is myth not history" (314). Mauberley also prefers myth to history, as we have seen, because myth allows him to construct an ideal world independent of the constraints of reality.

Even smaller details reinforce this symmetry between fascist aesthetics and Mauberley's framing of his story. Sontag notes that mountain climbing in Nazi films was "a visually irresistible metaphor for unlimited aspiration toward the high mystic goal, both beautiful and terrifying, which was later to become concrete in Führer-worship" (307). Mauberley's flight up the mountain to the Grand Elysium Hotel, climbing into Austria, seems a parody of such symbolism. Earlier, at Nauly, contemplating suicide by drowning, he thinks: ". . . I had always promised myself: before death — height. And before height, surely some sense of climbing . . ." (312). This is the aesthetic by which he lives and dies. It explains his attraction to the Duchess of Windsor. He confides: "it was her audacity that won me. Her ruthless stillness. . . . It was not and it has not been a fearful thing to watch her climb" (75). That awkwardly worded sentence seems defensive, and no wonder. She has climbed over the dead bodies of good men, such as Ned Allenby, and of innocent children, such as Maria da Gama. Mauberley knows that even he will eventually be sacrificed for her climb. As a study in misplaced idealism, his story is both sad and chilling. Although Williams sees only his voyeurism and exhibitionism, it is this misguided idealism that makes it impossible to condemn him out of hand.

Similarly, Mauberley's naming Hugo, the boy assigned to him as a servant, *"die weisse Ratte"* (28), while playfully taking Herr Kachelmeyer at his word when he first denies that the noises that Mauberley hears are made by other people, also seems to parody the derogatory image of rats that Hitler used to characterize the Jews in his racist propaganda. Such a naming dehumanizes and is therefore deeply troubling when it is recalled in what seems an ironic invocation by the frame narrator in describing Reinhardt's murder of all survivors after he has finished with Mauberley. He kills "The ratty father; the terrified mother; the running, squealing children" (388). But far from justifying their annihilation, as Hitler intended in his use of the rat as a symbol of the Jew, the dehumanizing language in Findley's narrative poignantly reinforces the tragedy of these deaths by juxtaposing the urge to live with Reinhardt's compulsion to destroy. The language of the white rat, however, also reminds us that Reinhardt's viciousness is legally sanctioned and encouraged by the Nazi regime. There is a context for his evil that goes beyond the individual into the social sphere. He is not an aberration but the logical expression of the fascist system, which Mauberley endorses until his recantation in his final testament.

Findley therefore seems to invoke a fascist aesthetic in the novel specifically to counter it and to question its cultural authority (while not always remaining immune to what he finds fascinating in it). Many of his invocations of fascist aesthetics appear in the form of parody. Hutcheon argues, however, that

> parody is as compromised as it is potentially revolutionary: it always acknowledges the power of that which it parodies, even as it challenges it. And this is, of course, what makes it such an attractive mode for postmodernism's paradoxically complicitous critique. (*Canadian Postmodern* 110–11)

Certainly, Findley's text acknowledges the power, even the seductiveness, of a fascist aesthetic in the course of challenging it as morally wrong. The debate about whether or not that acknowledgement makes his work complicitous with what it critiques has mostly taken place within a larger discussion of the strengths and weaknesses of postmodernist literary practices.

According to Craig Owens, "postmodernism is usually treated, by its protagonists and antagonists alike, as a crisis of cultural authority, specifically of the authority vested in Western European culture and its institutions" (57). This definition seems particularly well suited to Findley's concern in *Famous Last Words* that Dachau and Hiroshima represent the suicide of Western civilization, a suicide presaged, perhaps, by Mauberley's father's leap into death and confirmed by both the king's abdication and Mauberley's submission to Reinhardt. That "crisis of cultural authority," indicated by postmodernist techniques throughout the text, is perhaps best summed up in Findley's playful imagining of the discomfiture of the statue of Christopher Columbus looking back in the direction "from which he had come so long ago" and asking, *"What have I done to deserve this end?"* His question poses part of the answer. In describing Nassau as *"Nowhere"* (268), he illustrates the Eurocentric assumptions that contemporary postcolonialism and postmodernism are questioning from different cultural starting points. The cultural certainties that justified Columbus's explorations and conquests are now under attack. Columbus, the imperialist, thought that his conquest and annihilation of other peoples was justified, and for five hundred years he was honoured for it. *Famous Last Words* implies that he was the product of the same kind of cultural certainty that produced American capitalism and European fascism. Once a hero, he is now perceived to be a villain. Mauberley expresses bewilderment over the same situation: once fêted, he is now ostracized. He chose the wrong side, Findley argues, but does he merit the end that he meets?

Many of the techniques that Findley employs in *Famous Last Words* have been identified as characteristic of literary postmodernism's assaults on the unity of conventional realist and modernist narratives and on the assumptions on which they relied. He employs quotation, parody, doubled structures, language games, self-reflexivity, gender ambiguity, typographical play such as a heavy reliance on italics, a cinematic style that leaps from scene to scene, and a confusing of the boundaries between fact and fiction, élite and popular culture. Each of these techniques destabilizes traditional certainties about how we make meaning.

In *A Poetics of Postmodernism*, Hutcheon asserts that postmodernism argues that "any meaning that exists is of our own creation" (43). Therefore, "it questions the very bases of any certainty (history, subjectivity, reference) and of any standards of judgment. Who sets them? When? Where? Why?" (57). She argues that the postmodern "reinstalls historical contexts as significant and even determining, but in so doing, it problematizes the entire notion of historical knowledge" (89). These statements describe the ways that *Famous Last Words* problematizes the context in which it puts writing on trial, but they cannot account for the moral urgency that this trial must be held despite the difficulty of establishing adequately grounded standards of judgement.

Unlike many postmodern texts, *Famous Last Words* questions the bases of certainty while insisting that such questioning cannot become an alibi for avoiding judgement or action, however provisional the taking of stands must be, given the changing nature of the demands that the world makes on us. Pennee argues that,

> though Findley's novels demonstrate that everything is a construction, it is clear through Mauberley's text that some constructions are — because their actual effects are less violent, less racist, less exclusionary, less fascist — preferable to others. It is also clear that such constructions can begin to function with the force of resistance to the dominant texts when they are brought into a different (personalized) focus. . . . (71)

For Pennee, then, Findley may problematize historical knowledge, but he does not turn that problematizing into an endless deferral of value judgements. Although there may be an initial problematizing of Mauberley's subjectivity through the fact that he has been borrowed from another writer's poem, and a certain problematizing of reference through the confusing of historical veracity, fictional mendacity, and fictional invention, both subjectivity and reference (what Pennee terms "a personalized focus" [71]) are ultimately employed in the novel to ground its appeal to our moral judgements.

Clive's statement in *The Wars* sums up the perspective that Findley seems to be trying to create in *Famous Last Words*: *"I doubt we'll ever be forgiven. All I hope is — they'll remember we were human beings"* (185). Such a perspective depends on a shared valuing of human life, something that the Nazis, the Fascists, and their collaborators clearly did not share. Pure postmodernists would presumably be more interested in questioning the grounds for such a direct appeal to experience and common sense, but Findley seems less intellectually rigorous in his adherence to exposing contradictions and maintaining a sceptical stance. Ultimately, he appears more of an old-fashioned moralist employing contemporary postmodernist techniques to his own (sometimes ambiguous) ends.

Yet postmodernist techniques, as Hutcheon often points out, carry their own ideological implications, which cannot simply be wished away. In a persuasive meditation, Dean MacCannell wonders whether the defeat of what he calls "strong" or "hard" fascism at the end of the Second World War actually paved the way for "the founding of soft fascism, which no longer needs to use physical force to achieve its goals" (186). This seems to be the kind of argument that Freyberg develops at the end of *Famous Last Words*, when he despairs of his side maintaining its vigilance or continuing its resistance to fascist ideas now that the formal battles have been won.

MacCannell's descriptions of postmodern soft fascism sometimes seem uncannily accurate as an account of Mauberley's motivations in joining with fascists originally. According to MacCannell,

> The only permissible postmodern desire is for *attention* or *fame*, and not fame for any specific accomplishment. It is a new, pure kind of fame without subject or predicate, like the kind of sensation that might be derived from being admired while riding in someone else's Mercedes Benz. (220)

Findley has Dorothy Pound think similar thoughts as she helps Mauberley prepare to flee near the end of the war: "Dorothy thought of all the photos over the years of Mauberley printed in the papers and the magazines. Seen with this one and that one and everyone. He'd wanted that. And got it. Now he would pay for it" (8).

Perhaps that final point marks both Findley's distance from his character and the later Mauberley's distance from his earlier self. Whereas neither fascism nor postmodernism cares to pay the price for its moral decisions, because each in its own way questions the basis of morality on which such a logic rests, Findley (like a true Canadian) is still interested in moral costs and in the consequences of choice.

In arguing that postmodernist writing is an explication of soft fascism, MacCannell notes the following as "points of correspondence" between them:

> the death drive, the attack on the notion of truth as so much metaphysical baggage, the sense of living in an infinite instant at the end of history, nostalgia for the folk-primitive-peasant, schizophrenia at the level of culture, and general ennui periodically interrupted by euphoric release from all constraint. All these are named characteristics of both classic fascism and postmodern aesthetics. (187)

This list describes elements of Mauberley's character and narrative, and of *Famous Last Words* as a whole, tendencies that they flirt with but ultimately, I think, wish to reject. Nonetheless, this affinity between the styles of fascism and postmodernism helps us to see Findley's style in *Famous Last Words* as more problematic than it might first appear. MacCannell points out that "The best way to keep a cultural form alive is to pretend to be revealing its secrets while keeping its secrets" (196). This insight seems uncannily close to describing what is hidden and revealed in Mauberley's testament. If he is revealing the secrets of the Nazis, why is there so much on the failed Penelope cabal and so little on the hugely successful (from the Nazi point of view) death camps, unethical scientific experiments, tortures, propaganda successes, rallies, or even on the reasons for his initial involvement with fascism or the role that he plays in its rise, which leads to Julia Franklin's attacks? In the absence of evidence for Mauberley's importance in the movement, her animosity seems unnecessary. And we learn of Dachau through Freyberg and Quinn, not from Mauberley.

There is also the question of why the novel expends so much energy on psychological explanations of one individual's attraction to fascism and devotes so little attention to political, social, or philosophical explanations of the fascist success in attracting intellectuals to its cause. In presenting this explanation of Mauberley's fascism, *Famous*

Last Words repeats what MacCannell terms "the average Nazi's self-image": "Adherents to National Socialism specifically chose not to understand it in political terms" (206). Mauberley and his friends avoid political talk: "It had always been a laughing time and the talk was always gossip, never work and never, never politics . . ." (30).

To counter such a view, to return to political specifics is necessary. But Findley chooses to oppose what he sees as fascist inhumanity by celebrating a universal notion of the human, grounded in the body and its desire for survival. Although the novel is loaded with dates and details from history, his notion of fascism seems equally universalized, in a manner made familiar by contemporary critics such as Barthes, Debord, Eco, Guattari, and Derrida. According to Mac-Cannell, those postmodernist thinkers suggest that "the only escape [from fascism] is to draw an arbitrary line and leap across, imprisoning fascism forever in 'history' or in the unconscious" (202). This is one way of describing *Famous Last Words*, which tries to relegate fascism to a prison of words constructed of historical narrative and psychic need.

Perhaps Findley chooses this route because fascism is not really on trial in the novel. It has been judged guilty in advance. What the novel needs to explore is literature's possible complicity in such an ideology. Is every document of civilization also a document of barbarism, as Benjamin claims? Is language inherently fascist, as Barthes suggests? The novel reinforces the standard Western condemnation of fascism in order to focus its interrogation on other issues. What role can art and the artist play in preventing a fascist revival? What role did writing play — and could it play it again — in promoting fascism? Mauberley is no Schindler, risking his life to save others from the gas chambers. Can his confession be seen at all as a comparable act of resistance? Findley clearly wishes to argue that literature not only urges action but is also a form of action in its own right. Yet each model of heroism put forward in the novel seems a doomed gesture of resistance. The words of Luis Quintana, Isabella Loverso, Lorenzo de Broca, Ned Allenby, and finally Mauberley himself express a resistance that fails to change much but that Findley argues is nonetheless necessary.

These individual acts of resistance seem meant to be applauded in the context set up by *Famous Last Words*. Yet we can see that they fail for two reasons. First, they take the form of symbolic gestures rather than of actions directed toward changing material reality. The assumption behind them is that intervention in the field of representation can directly change how people think, feel, and, ultimately, act. But Mauberley's story shows the falsity of this assumption even as he continues to hope that it is true. Second, they are based on the view than an individual may act alone to change history. All Mauberley's heroes are individualists. The Resistance as a movement is absent from the text. Findley's ideology celebrates isolated, and often idiosyncratic, individual gestures of protest, which often lend themselves, like Robert Ross's saving the horses in *The Wars*, to misinterpretation. Although the novel repeatedly shows the self-deception implicit in such an excessive valorization of individualism, particularly in the account of the Spitfire Bazaar, its sympathy for Mauberley betrays a sympathy for this position. Neither Mauberley nor Findley seems capable of imagining a community-based form of resistance.

Instead, *Famous Last Words* locates a site of resistance in the power of the imagination to bridge distances between people. In the abstract, such a valorizing of the imagination may seem hopelessly idealistic, but the novel demonstrates, through Quinn and Freyberg, how communally shared reading may begin to clear a space for dialogue. *Famous Last Words* resists the demonization of the other, showing, instead, the ordinariness of evil. Fascism is not the monstrous other: it is shown to exist here and now because its seeds live in our culture and literary tradition. The novel is a study in complicity. It shows what it is like for the privileged to live under fascism, how it creeps up on us and changes us before we know it. By evading simplistic models of good versus evil, Findley makes it harder for us to distance ourselves from the inside view that Mauberley provides of what it feels like to be a collaborator.

Psychologism

Mauberley is not only a collaborator. He is also an expatriate, someone who lives abroad with no commitments anywhere. His relationships are mostly superficial, and all his ties to others have been broken by the end of his story, except for his sadomasochistic tie to Reinhardt, who fearlessly expresses Mauberley's own most antisocial urges. What conclusions are we to draw from a text that asks us to see such a man as a potential hero?

Findley's depiction of Mauberley conforms to the pattern in Canadian literature that Larry McDonald identifies as psychologism. McDonald employs Russell Jacoby's definition of the term: "the reduction of social concepts to individual and psychological ones" (128). Symptoms include tendencies that I have already identified in Findley's style: "Political movements such as nationalism and socialism are presented to the reader as nothing but symptoms of psychological disruption" (131); history is presented as "essentially determined by consciousness," and "a change in individual consciousness (a quasi-religious rebirth) is the only legitimate history-making activity open to us." McDonald reiterates this last important point: "History is not something their protagonists work to change or make; it is something to be watched, something that is carefully arranged in the novels so that the characters can learn to see how they ought to see it" (142). He deplores such a project because he believes that it "amounts to an uncritical promotion of political resignation and psychological adaptation" (143), not to the promotion of searching for collective solutions to contemporary problems.

Famous Last Words lends itself to such an interpretation. What redeems it, in my view, is its depiction of scenes of reading as a collective activity that moves writing beyond the private sphere into the public realm. *Famous Last Words* seeks to renew the imagination. Through Mauberley's failures, it implies that this renewal must come through enlarging the sphere allowed to individual human beings for making history beyond the traditionally limited space of observing the powerful and trying to stay out of their way. Mauberley's triumph is not finding his voice as a writer but articulating the limitations of such a circumscribed view of writing's potential.

The Canadian Context

Although Sir Harry Oakes is the only Canadian character in the novel (and even he was born in the United States), a Canadian wrote *Famous Last Words*, and it addresses Canadian concerns from a Canadian context of debate. That context is attuned to international influences, but it has its own sense of cultural space and perspective.

Findley's point is that Canadian concerns are now largely global: war and peace, fascism and antifascism, individual and community, "A generation of children . . . that carries guns . . ." (35). When Mauberley's "boxed set of wars" pulled down "all the old necessities for literature; all the old prescriptions for use of the written word; all the old traditions of order and articulation fading under the roar of bombast and rhetoric" (5), Canadian writers also became implicated in discovering new ways to make literature relevant to our lives. To the Canadian who felt excluded from those old traditions or at best marginalized within them, such a change became an opportunity.

Findley's irreverence toward the Duke and Duchess of Windsor, Hollywood icons, and the American dream seems to function as a kind of declaration of cultural independence. Canadians know these myths, but they are only partially ours. Mauberley's voyeurism and fifth-businesslike role in the narrative seem expressions of a Canadian cultural stance that, *Famous Last Words* suggests, has outlived its usefulness. It is time to play a more active role in making our own history and writing our own stories.

The book ends with Quinn dating Mauberley's epilogue as if to freeze it in the past, but Freyberg's insistence that we must not forget what Mauberley's narrative excludes cannot be so easily contained. When Quinn finishes reading Mauberley's testament, he thinks: "Two worlds; and now the horror was over in both of them" (389). But Freyberg immediately proves him wrong. The horrors of Dachau live and must be remembered, everywhere, by everyone. They live seared into human bodies and human memories; they are documented in pictures and in writing. When the two men touch, however briefly, after this last exchange, Quinn is acknowledging not just Freyberg's personal pain but also the validity in his insistence that these events must never be forgotten.

". . . Captain Freyberg's attitude towards the Nazis was a matter of concern" to the authorities who wish to forget (392); it is a matter of concern to Findley because he wishes us to remember, especially, perhaps, those of us in Canada who were insulated from the worst of what happened but whose lives have been affected nonetheless. The worst danger, in his eyes, is to imagine ourselves immune. That complacency is what lulls the fleeing Germans into an illusion of safety on Mauberley's train at the beginning of the novel: "The S.S. always came in the dark for others. Now, they were splitting open the dark, reaching in through the dreams for the dreamers. Down. Out. Down. Out. It was terrible" (16). *Famous Last Words* performs a similar assault on Canadian complacency and on the mistaken belief that Europe's problems have nothing to do with us.

The myth of Canadian innocence poses a danger particularly tempting to those of us who have inherited a national mythology that calls our nation "a peaceable kingdom" and insists that we have no past with which to come to terms. *Famous Last Words* tells us that Europe's past, and implicitly its imperialist presence and capitalist legacy in America, are our past. If we are to understand this history, then we must reenter it imaginatively through literature. Those "famous last words" are the dying gasps of our cultural heritage, and if we wish to survive, we must listen to, and learn from, them.

Hutcheon points out that, for *Famous Last Words*, reading is more than voyeurism; it is "an act in itself, an act that brings to life words on a wall or a page . . . ; through reading, the word is figuratively made flesh" (*Canadian Postmodern* 64). This might seem a sophisticated reiteration of McDonald's point about spiritual rebirth offered in place of real agency for change beyond the private realm. Yet Hutcheon is right in insisting that reading itself can unlock an awareness of our potential for action in the world. The very debate in the novel about how to read Mauberley suggests to me that his passivity and sense of helplessness are thrown into question rather than advocated. *Famous Last Words* rests its case in the defence of literature on its ability to perform this testing and transformative function. Words had a real impact in making fascism acceptable in the 1930s and 1940s. Findley hopes that his words may prove an equally strong force in reminding us of our past, strengthening our resolve, and helping us to imagine a better future. He has written a complex novel that ensures, through the debates that it has generated, that the final words on its significance are likely never to be written, for new readers will advance fresh interpretations and new angles for understanding the challenges that literature continues to pose to life, and life to literature. Paradoxically, *Famous Last Words* makes last words impossible and more words inevitable.

Works Cited

Barthes, Roland. *Mythologies*. Trans. Annette Lavers. 1972. London: Granada-Paladin, 1973.

Benjamin, Walter. "Theses on the Philosophy of History." *Illuminations*. By Benjamin. Ed. Hannah Arendt. Trans. Harry Zohn. 1968. New York: Schocken, 1985. 253–64.

Benson, Eugene. " 'Whispers of Chaos': *Famous Last Words*." *World Literature Written in English* 21 (1982): 599–606.

Brydon, Diana. "Timothy Findley: A Post-Holocaust, Post-Colonial Vision." *International Literature in English: Essays on the Major Writers*. Ed. Robert L. Ross. New York: Garland, 1991. 583–92.

Cameron, Elspeth. "After the Wars." Rev. of *Famous Last Words*. *Saturday Night* Jan. 1982: 53–54.

Coetzee, J.M. "Interview" [part of "Autobiography and Confession" sec.]. With David Attwell. *Doubling the Point: Essays and Interviews*. By Coetzee. Ed. Attwell. Cambridge: Harvard UP, 1992. 243–50.

Dellamora, Richard. "Becoming-Homosexual/Becoming-Canadian: Ironic Voice and the Politics of Location in Timothy Findley's *Famous Last Words*." *Double Talking: Essays on Verbal and Visual Ironies in Canadian Contemporary Art and Literature*. Ed. Linda Hutcheon. Toronto: ECW, 1992. 172–200.

Duffy, Dennis. "Let Us Compare Histories: Meaning and Mythology in Findley's *Famous Last Words*." *Essays on Canadian Writing* 30 (1984–85): 187–205.

——. *Sounding the Iceberg: An Essay on Canadian Historical Novels*. Toronto: ECW, 1986.

Findley, Timothy. *Famous Last Words*. Toronto: Clarke, 1981.

——. *Inside Memory: Pages from a Writer's Workbook*. Toronto: Harper Collins, 1990.

——. Interview. With Terry Goldie. *Kunapipi* 6.1 (1984): 56–67.

——. "Interview with Timothy Findley." With Jeffrey Canton. *Paragraph* 15.1 (1993): 3–7.

——. " 'Long Live the Dead': An Interview with Timothy Findley." With Johan Aitken. *Journal of Canadian Fiction* 33 (1982): 79–93.

———. "My Final Hour: An Address to the Philosophy Society, Trent University, Monday, 26 January 1987." *Journal of Canadian Studies* 22.1 (1987): 5–16.

———. "Timothy Findley: The Marvel of Reality." With Bruce Meyer and Brian O'Riordan. *In Their Words: Interviews with Fourteen Canadian Writers.* Toronto: Anansi, 1984. 45–54.

———. *The Wars.* Toronto: Clarke, 1977.

Fraser, G.S. *Ezra Pound.* Writers and Critics. Glasgow: Oliver, 1962.

Garebian, Keith. Rev. of *Famous Last Words. Quarry Magazine* 31.3 (1982): 93–97.

Gill, John. "The King and I." *Time Out* [London] 25 Mar.–1 Apr. 1987: 28.

Gold, Ivan. "Dropping Names." Rev. of *Famous Last Words. New York Times Book Review* 15 Aug. 1982: 10.

Hair, Donald. "To Catch the Reader Unaware." Rev. of *Famous Last Words. Brick* 17 (1983): 8–14.

Hamilton, Alastair. Introduction. *The Appeal of Fascism: A Study of Intellectuals and Fascism 1919–1945.* London: Blond, 1971. xv–xxiii.

Hatlen, Burton. "Ezra Pound and Fascism." *Ezra Pound and History.* Ed. Marianne Korn. Ezra Pound Scholarship Series. Orono, ME: Foundation, U of Maine, 1985. 145–72.

Howells, Coral Ann. " 'History as She Is Never Writ': *The Wars* and *Famous Last Words.*" *Kunapipi* 6.1 (1984): 49–56.

Hulcoop, John F. "The Will to Be." Rev. of *Famous Last Words. Canadian Literature* (1982): 117–22.

Hutcheon, Linda. "Canadian Historiographic Metafiction." *Essays on Canadian Writing* 30 (1984–85): 228–38.

———. *The Canadian Postmodern: A Study of Contemporary English-Canadian Fiction.* Toronto: Oxford UP, 1988.

———. *A Poetics of Postmodernism: History, Theory, Fiction.* New York: Routledge, 1988.

———. *The Politics of Postmodernism.* New Accents. London: Routledge, 1989.

Ingham, David. "Bashing the Fascists: The Moral Dimensions of Findley's Fiction." *Studies in Canadian Literature* 15.2 (1990): 33–54.

Kazin, Alfred. "Homer to Mussolini: The Fascination and Terror of Ezra Pound." *Ezra Pound: The Legacy of Kulchur.* Ed. Marcel Smith and William A. Ulmer. Tuscaloosa: U of Alabama P, 1988. 25–50.

Kermode, Frank. "A Royal Coup." Rev. of *Famous Last Words. Guardian* [London] 20 Mar. 1987: 13.

Kuester, Martin. *Framing Truths: Parodic Structures in Contemporary English-Canadian Historical Novels.* Theory/Culture Series 12. Toronto: U of Toronto P, 1992.

Lacoue-Labarthe, Philippe, and Jean-Luc Nancy. "The Nazi Myth." Trans. Brian Holmes. *Critical Inquiry* 16 (1990): 291–312.

Lehmann-Haupt, Christopher. "Books of the Times." Rev. of *Famous Last Words*. *New York Times* 22 June 1982: C10.

MacCannell, Dean. *Empty Meeting Grounds: The Tourist Papers*. London: Routledge, 1992.

McDonald, Larry. "Psychologism and the Philosophy of Progress: The Recent Fiction of MacLennan, Davies and Atwood." *Studies in Canadian Literature* 9 (1984): 121–43.

Melmoth, John. "The Off-the-Wall Writing on the Wall." Rev. of *Famous Last Words*. *Times Literary Supplement* 24 Apr. 1987: 435.

Miller, Owen. "Intertextual Identity." *Identity of the Literary Text*. Ed. Mario Valdés and Miller. Toronto: U of Toronto P, 1985. 19–40.

Moon, Barbara. "Fixing the Books." *Saturday Night* Aug. 1983: 55–58.

New, W.H. Introduction. "Canada." *Journal of Commonwealth Literature* 17.2 (1982): 52.

Owens, Craig. "The Discourse of Others: Feminists and Postmodernism." *Postmodern Culture*. Ed. Hal Foster. London: Pluto, 1983. 57–82.

Pearlman, Daniel. "The Anti-Semitism of Ezra Pound." Rev. of *"Ezra Pound Speaking": Radio Speeches of World War II*, ed. Leonard W. Doob. *Contemporary Literature* 22.1 (1981): 104–15.

Pennee, Donna Palmateer. *Moral Metafiction: Counterdiscourse in the Novels of Timothy Findley*. Toronto: ECW, 1991.

Pound, Ezra. *Hugh Selwyn Mauberley*. *Selected Poems*. New Directions Paperbook 66. New York: New Directions, 1957. 61–77.

Reed, J.D. "Atrocities." *Time* 2 Aug. 1982: 54.

Ruthven, K.K. *A Guide to Ezra Pound's "Personae" (1926)*. Berkeley: U of California P, 1969.

Schieder, Rupert. "Irritating and Fascinating." Rev. of *Famous Last Words*. *Canadian Forum* Feb. 1982: 36–37.

Scobie, Stephen. "Eye-Deep in Hell: Ezra Pound, Timothy Findley, and Hugh Selwyn Mauberley." *Essays on Canadian Writing* 30 (1984–85): 206–27.

Seddon, Elizabeth. "The Reader as Actor in the Novels of Timothy Findley." *Future Indicative: Literary Theory and Canadian Literature*. Ed. John Moss. Reappraisals: Canadian Writers 13. Ottawa: U of Ottawa P, 1987. 213–20.

Shields, E.F. "Mauberley's Lies: Fact and Fiction in Timothy Findley's *Famous Last Words*." *Journal of Canadian Studies* 22.4 (1987–88): 44–59.

——. " 'The Perfect Voice': Mauberley as Narrator in Timothy Findley's *Famous Last Words*." *Canadian Literature* 119 (1988): 84–98.

Sontag, Susan. "Fascinating Fascism." *A Susan Sontag Reader*. New York: Farrar, 1982. 305–25.

Surette, Leon. "Pound, Postmodernism, and Fascism." *University of Toronto Quarterly* 59 (1989–90): 334–55.

Tonkin, Boyd. "Hitler's Understudy." Rev. of *Famous Last Words*. *New Statesman* 27 Mar. 1987: 33.

Walton, Priscilla. " 'This Isn't a Fairy Tale. . . . It's Mythology': The Colonial Perspective in *Famous Last Words.*" *Commonwealth* 14.1 (1991): 9–15.

Williams, David. *Confessional Fictions: A Portrait of the Artist in the Canadian Novel.* Toronto: U of Toronto P, 1991.

York, Lorraine M. *Front Lines: The Fiction of Timothy Findley.* Toronto: ECW, 1991.

———. *"The Other Side of Dailiness": Photography in the Works of Alice Munro, Timothy Findley, Michael Ondaatje, and Margaret Laurence.* Toronto: ECW, 1988.

Index